Virgil *Aeneid* XI

The following titles are available from Bloomsbury for the OCR specifications in Latin and Greek for examinations from June 2019 to June 2021

Apuleius *Metamorphoses* **V: A Selection**, with introduction, commentary notes and vocabulary by Stuart Thomson

Cicero *Philippic* **II: A Selection**, with introduction, commentary notes and vocabulary by Christopher Tanfield

Horace *Odes*: **A Selection**, with introduction, commentary notes and vocabulary by John Godwin

Horace *Satires*: **A Selection**, with introduction, commentary notes and vocabulary by John Godwin

Ovid *Amores* **II: A Selection**, with introduction, commentary notes and vocabulary by Alfred Artley

Tacitus *Histories* **I: A Selection**, with introduction by Ellen O'Gorman and commentary notes and vocabulary by Benedict Gravell

Virgil *Aeneid* **XI: A Selection**, with introduction, commentary notes and vocabulary by Ashley Carter

OCR Anthology for Classical Greek AS and A Level, covering the prescribed texts by Aristophanes, Euripides, Herodotus, Homer, Plato and Xenophon, with introduction, commentary notes and vocabulary by Stephen P. Anderson, Rob Colborn, Neil Croally, Charlie Paterson, Chris Tudor and Claire Webster

Supplementary resources for these volumes can be found at www.bloomsbury.com/OCR-editions-2019–2021
Please type the URL into your web browser and follow the instructions to access the Companion Website. If you experience any problems, please contact Bloomsbury at academicwebsite@bloomsbury.com

Virgil *Aeneid* XI:
A Selection

Lines 1–224, 498–521, 532–596, 648–689, 725–835

With introduction, commentary notes and
vocabulary by Ashley Carter

BLOOMSBURY ACADEMIC
LONDON • NEW YORK • OXFORD • NEW DELHI • SYDNEY

BLOOMSBURY ACADEMIC
Bloomsbury Publishing Plc
50 Bedford Square, London, WC1B 3DP, UK

BLOOMSBURY, BLOOMSBURY ACADEMIC and the Diana logo are trademarks of
Bloomsbury Publishing Plc

First published in Great Britain 2018

Cover image: charistoone-images / Alamy Stock Photo

A catalogue record for this book is available from the British Library.

Library of Congress Cataloging-in-Publication Data
Names: Virgil, author. | Carter, Ashley, editor, writer of added commentary.
Title: Aeneid XI : a selection, lines 1–224, 498–521, 532–596, 648–689,725–835 / with
introduction, commentary notes and vocabulary by Ashley Carter.
Description: London ; New York : Bloomsbury Academic, an imprint of
Bloomsbury Publishing Plc, 2018. | Text in Latin, with introduction and
commentary notes in English. | Includes bibliographical references.
Identifiers: LCCN 2017049464| ISBN 9781350008373 (pbk.) | ISBN 9781350008397 (epdf)
Subjects: LCSH: Virgil. Aeneis.
Classification: LCC PA6803.B31 C37 2018 | DDC 873/.01–dc23 LC record available at
https://lccn.loc.gov/2017049464

ISBN: PB   978-1-3500-0837-3
ePDF: 978-1-3500-0839-7
eBook: 978-1-3500-0838-0

Typeset by RefineCatch Limited, Bungay, Suffolk

To find out more about our authors and books visit www.bloomsbury.com
and sign up for our newsletters.

Contents

Preface

The text and notes found in this volume are designed to guide any student who has mastered Latin up to GCSE level and wishes to read a selection of Virgil's *Aeneid* XI in the original.

The edition is, however, particularly designed to support students who are reading Virgil's text in preparation for OCR's AS / A-Level Latin examination in June 2019–June 2021. (Please note this edition uses AS to refer indiscriminately to AS and the first year of A Level, i.e. Group 1.)

The text used is that of Williams (1973), suitably adjusted to suit the house style. There is one change to this text: in line 149 *Pallante* has been changed to *Pallanta*, in line with most editions.

This edition contains a detailed introduction to the context of the *Aeneid* XI. The notes to the book itself aim to help students bridge the gap between GCSE and AS Level Latin, and focus therefore on the harder points of grammar and word order and major stylistic points. At the end of the book is a full vocabulary list for all the words contained in the prescribed sections, with words in OCR's Defined Vocabulary List for AS Level Latin flagged by means of an asterisk.

The author is grateful both to the editorial staff at Bloomsbury for their help in planning this book and to the reviewer for a detailed list of helpful comments.

Ashley Carter
April 2017

Introduction

The *Aeneid*

The *Aeneid* is an epic poem in 12 books, totalling 9,896 lines. It tells the story of a Trojan prince, Aeneas, who survives the sack of Troy by the Greeks. He escapes with his son and father, and leads a large band of survivors across the Mediterranean Sea in search of a new home. He is guided on his way by his mother, the goddess Venus, and by various more or less obscure prophecies.

In Book I the fleet of ships is blown off course by the intervention of the goddess Juno, who is hostile to the Trojans and jealous of Venus. The scattered ships come to land on the shore of North Africa, where Aeneas is directed to the new city of Carthage, still being built by its queen, Dido. Dido welcomes the Trojans and lays on a dinner for them.

In Book II Dido persuades Aeneas to tell the story of his adventures. The whole book is devoted to his account of the sack of Troy following the acceptance of the wooden horse into the city. Aeneas escapes with his son and elderly father, but loses his wife on their way out of the city.

Book III covers Aeneas' account of the Trojans' journey from Troy to Carthage, including several attempts to settle on lands that they wrongly thought were intended for them by the prophecies. By the end of this book, they have a clearer idea of their true destination, Italy, but Aeneas' father dies.

In Book IV Dido entertains Aeneas and the other Trojan leaders with a hunting expedition. By this time she has fallen in love with Aeneas and, when a storm drives them to take shelter in a cave, they make love, which leads Dido to consider them married. Aeneas is tempted to stay, but the god Mercury brings a message to him from

Jupiter, telling him he must leave Carthage and pursue his allotted destiny. Aeneas can find no way to break the news to Dido; when she discovers his plans, she attempts in vain to make him change his mind. When he refuses, her love turns to anger and hostility, and finally she commits suicide as Aeneas sails away.

In Book V the Trojans sail from Carthage to Sicily (on their route to the west coast of Italy, which is where their destiny lies). In Sicily, Aeneas organizes funeral games to commemorate the anniversary of his father's death there on an earlier visit.

In Book VI the Trojans make landfall in Italy at Cumae (near Naples), where the Sibyl, a prophetess inspired by the god Apollo, leads Aeneas down into the Underworld. After passing by Tartarus, where the souls of the wicked are punished, they proceed through the fields of Elysium until they find the spirit of Aeneas' father, Anchises. Anchises is privileged (now he is dead) to know the future, and he introduces to his son a parade of the yet-to-be-born souls of many of the great figures from Roman history down to Virgil's own day, climaxing in Augustus. In this way Aeneas is reinvigorated with a determination to complete his mission.

Book VII takes the Trojans from Cumae to Latium, where they build a camp by the bank of the river Tiber. Aeneas sends some of his men in search of the local population; they come to a city, whose king is Latinus. Virgil never quite names Latinus' city, but implies that it is called Laurentum (as it will be called throughout this book for the sake of simplicity). Latinus initially welcomes the Trojans, suggesting a match between Aeneas and his daughter Lavinia. Juno, still hostile to the Trojans, ensures that Turnus, chief of a local tribe called the Rutuli, to whom Lavinia was already promised, refuses to accept the new arrangement. Turnus declares war on the Trojans and tries to persuade Latinus to support him.

In Book VIII Aeneas, in need of allies against the Rutuli and Latins, goes to Pallanteum, which lies on the site of the future Rome. There he has no difficulty persuading the king, Evander, to lend him an army under the command of his son, Pallas. Venus has a new shield made for her son by the god Vulcan. Aeneas admires the decoration on the shield, which contains many scenes of significant events from the future history of Rome.

In Book IX Turnus takes advantage of Aeneas' absence at Pallanteum to lay siege to the Trojan camp. Two young men, Nisus and Euryalus, volunteer to take a message through the enemy encirclement to Aeneas. Despite showing great valour, the two are killed. Turnus attacks the Trojan camp, even gaining access but, lacking support, he is forced to escape by jumping into the river.

In Book X Aeneas returns at the head of his reinforcements. Pallas excels in the ensuing battle but is no match for Turnus, who kills him and takes his sword-belt as a trophy. Aeneas, maddened by guilt and grief, wades into the enemy forces, killing large numbers of them, including Mezentius, a king allied to the Latins.

In Book XI Pallas is buried, amid the mourning of his father and the Trojans. After a truce to collect and bury the dead on both sides, fighting resumes, during which the warrior-maiden Camilla battles bravely for the Latins before being killed. The events of the book take up just four days: Pallas' funeral occupies the first; the second and third are devoted (briefly) to the truce and burials; the fourth, taking up the second half of the book, is concerned with Camilla's *aristeia* (a frequent component of epic poetry in which the focus is on the successes in battle of one individual, often preceding that person's death). Interestingly, Aeneas himself, after playing centre stage in the first half of this prescription, only makes one further, very brief, appearance at the end of the book.

In Book XII a single combat is arranged between Aeneas and Turnus in order to decide the outcome of the war. On Olympus the two goddesses are forced to come to an agreement, as a result of which Juno abandons her support of Turnus. In the combat, Aeneas wounds

Turnus and is tempted to spare his life, until he notices on his shoulder the sword-belt he had stripped from the body of Pallas. In a fit of anger Aeneas kills him.

Virgil's life

Publius Vergilius Maro, or Virgil as we now call him, was born on a farm near Mantua in Northern Italy in 70 BCE. After completing a full education in Rome, where he befriended many leading figures, he was driven by poor health and a preference for country life back to his father's farm. Unlike many educated Roman citizens, he did not pursue a public career in the army, politics or law courts, but decided to focus on poetry.

His first poems were the *Eclogues*, ten pastoral poems written over the course of five years and published in 37 BCE. It was during the period of their composition that his family was dispossessed of their farm by the authorities in Rome who needed land to settle army veterans. As a result Virgil moved to Campania (in the south of Italy), where he spent most of the rest of his life.

From 37 to 30 BCE Virgil occupied himself with composing the *Georgics*, a didactic poem in four books providing instruction in good farming techniques. He dedicated this poem to Maecenas, the close friend of Octavian, whose patronage he enjoyed for the rest of his life.

The success he achieved with these first two published works spurred Virgil on to compose what most have considered to be his greatest poem, the *Aeneid*. The emperor Augustus (as Octavian called himself from 27 BCE onward) at the very least supported his ambition and may well have commissioned the work. This was more or less complete but largely unrevised at the time of Virgil's death in 19 BCE, following the contraction of a fever while on a voyage to

Greece. In his will he left instructions for the manuscript of the *Aeneid* to be destroyed; Augustus, however, overrode them and saw to the publication of the poem.

The literary context of the *Aeneid*

Exactly what motivated Virgil to take on so huge a task is impossible now to establish with any certainty; we can only make deductions from the prevailing circumstances and from the little reliable information we are given by ancient sources (the most important of which are a biography written by either Aelius Donatus or Suetonius, and the commentary of Servius, both written long after Virgil's death).

One circumstance that Virgil must have been very aware of was the lack of a Roman equivalent of Homer's Greek epic poems, the *Iliad* and the *Odyssey*. These two poems were composed probably in the eighth or seventh centuries BCE and certainly long before the splendours of the Greek classical period, by which time Homer's works had taken on the roles that Shakespeare and the holy books of the great religions play in our society today. Even seven hundred years later in Virgil's day the two poems formed a sort of cultural bedrock upon which the foundations of the Roman cultural tradition were built. Unfortunately, though, Rome had no part herself in these poems, being probably no more than a small settlement beyond the fringes of the Greek world at the time they were composed.

There had been a few attempts to emulate Homer with later epic poems, both in the Greek world (in particular the *Argonautica* of Apollonius of Rhodes) and among the Romans (Ennius' historical epic is now lost but Lucretius's *De Rerum Natura*, a philosophical work, has survived and was familiar to Virgil). No work, however, filled the gap in Roman culture that the absence of a Homer caused. Rome had by Virgil's time eclipsed Greece politically and militarily and was trying hard to equal that country's literary, philosophical and artistic achievement. There was, in fact, a huge output of creative works, at first simply copying or translating Greek originals, then adapting them to Roman needs, and finally (in the view of some critics) surpassing them. This impetus to attain a high cultural standard may be seen in all genres of literature, painting, sculpture, architecture, philosophy and town-planning. Thus, all the great writers of Rome's Golden Age to a greater or lesser degree looked back to Greek writers for their inspiration. Virgil therefore had no reason to expect any criticism for modelling his *Aeneid* on Homer's originals; criticism would only be levelled at any failure to match the high standard set by Homer. In the event the *Aeneid* received the highest praise from all quarters; today many would argue that it represents the pinnacle of Rome's literary output.

Virgil modelled many characters and events throughout the *Aeneid* on the *Iliad* and *Odyssey*, and Book XI is no exception. Thus, any reader approaching the *Aeneid* who has a familiarity with the Homeric epics will gain an extra level of appreciation of it; this is as true today as it was in the time of Augustus. The shaping of one text by including references to other texts is called intertextuality, and there have been many studies of this element of the *Aeneid*. In this book the Commentary will make occasional references to intertextuality, but will allow for the fact that few users of this book are likely to be already familiar with Homer. Anyone wanting to pursue this further should consult Gransden (see Further reading).

The political context of the *Aeneid*

A second motivating factor for Virgil was the political environment in which he lived. The first century BCE had witnessed a succession of powerful individuals, usually army commanders, challenging senatorial authority and, in several cases, seizing power in Rome. The senate, historically the dominant force in the government, had always shared its power with individual statesmen, who, through a combination of wealth, popularity and birth, were able to get themselves elected to a succession of magistracies culminating in the consulship. The trouble was that the highest two of these magistracies carried with them the promise of lucrative provincial governorships and the command of one or more legions, sometimes indeed a whole army, if Rome happened to be at war. This system provided ambitious men with all the resources they needed to challenge the senate for political supremacy. As a result, there had been a succession of civil wars, with legion fighting against legion, each resulting in the seizure of power by an individual.

When Virgil was a young adult, Julius Caesar had defeated Pompey in an empire-wide civil war, but enjoyed less than five years of power before he was assassinated by a group of senators desperate to restore the authority of the senate. Unfortunately for them the senate was by this time too weak to reassert itself; further civil wars broke out, firstly between Caesar's assassins and his heirs, Mark Antony and Octavian, and then between the heirs themselves. These wars came to an end with the defeat of Mark Antony at the battle of Actium in 31 BCE, followed by his suicide. Octavian now found himself the virtually undisputed master of Rome and the empire, with a subservient senate able only to make a show of supporting him.

Octavian was both ambitious and wise enough to realize that the best future for both himself and Rome was for him to continue to exercise power; it was also clear to him that his only hope of achieving this was to win the full support of all sections of society, i.e. the senate, the people and the army. Since his adoptive father, Julius Caesar, had paid the price for seeking absolute power too overtly, he realized that success would depend on several stratagems: first, he must disguise the full extent of his authority by refusing any offer of absolute power while sharing standard magisterial powers with senators; secondly, he would emphasize the benefits of the peace that he, by ending the series of civil wars, had brought to the empire; thirdly, he would remind people of the greatness of Rome, to restore their pride and the moral standards that had plummeted during the waning decades of the Republic.

Whereas the first of these strategies was something that Octavian could achieve only by exercising his own political astuteness, the other two could be boosted by the publication of a grand epic poem which would portray Rome as the natural successor of the Greek Golden Age and with contemporary Rome as the climax of a new Golden Age. It is no surprise, therefore, that Augustus quickly persuaded Virgil to go ahead with his plan for an epic. All Virgil had to do was to find ways to glorify Rome and Octavian without compromising poetic integrity. The stage was set, therefore, for Virgil to begin his great work in 30 or 29 BCE. During the ten years or so that Virgil devoted to the composition, Octavian succeeded in strengthening his position of dominance to the extent that, by the time of Virgil's death, there was no longer a pressing need for propaganda; but Augustus and his wife Livia had been so moved by the excerpts that Virgil had read to them that they became determined to see the work published.

The mythological context of the *Aeneid*

Virgil needed a theme capable of linking Homer's Greek Golden Age to his own times. Among the many legends drawn on by Homer and later Greek writers was that of Aeneas. He was a prince of Dardania, a city neighbouring Troy, the son of Anchises and the goddess Venus; Anchises himself was a second cousin of Priam, the king of Troy. In the *Iliad*, Aeneas played a minor role fighting bravely but with limited success on the Trojan side during the Trojan War. More importantly, he was one of the few princes to escape the sack of Troy by the Greeks. In the centuries following Homer, the legends surrounding Aeneas expanded. It is impossible for us to know exactly when the legend began to include a voyage to the west coast of Italy, at the head of a large band of Trojan survivors; but this is the legend that Virgil inherited. There appear to have been several variants of this legend that a number of Roman writers, both historians and poets, had already included in their works. Thus, Virgil had a relatively free hand in adapting the myth to his own needs.

Long current in Rome was the story of Romulus, the legendary founder of the city. He was the son of Mars, and so provided Rome with a glorious foundation. Unfortunately, the traditional date of this foundation was 753 BCE, more than three hundred years later than the date ascribed by ancient historians to the Trojan War, i.e. to the time of Aeneas. This presented Virgil with a chronological gap that he would have to fill if he were to link successfully the two legends of Aeneas and Romulus so as to provide a smooth sequence of events from the Greek Golden Age to his own times.

Another, completely separate story was that of Dido, the legendary founder of Carthage, on the North African coast. According to the legend, she had fled from Tyre (a city on the coast of what is now Lebanon) to save her life; she was accompanied by enough citizens to provide the nucleus of her new city. Archaeological evidence suggests that Dido was a historical rather than a mythical figure, but places her in the late ninth century BCE, far too late to have played a role in the story of Aeneas (unless the Greek Dark Age theory is discarded, as some scholars now argue). Virgil may have inherited the idea of a liaison between Dido and Aeneas, or he may have invented it himself. For Virgil, Dido's involvement served two purposes: to link the three Punic Wars (fought between Rome and Carthage in the third and second centuries BCE and marking the beginning of Rome's overseas empire) with his central theme; and to bring out elements of Aeneas' character that would otherwise have been missing.

Virgil also had available various myths relating to the origins of cities near Rome, together with their rulers. These include Turnus and Latinus, who opposed the Trojan settlement in Italy, and Evander, who helped the Trojans.

These were the major sources upon which Virgil drew when stitching together his great theme. But equally important were the two poems of Homer. From these Virgil borrowed events, characters, language, stylistic features (such as the epic simile) and the close association of the gods with human affairs. Throughout the *Aeneid* echoes of Homer can be found. These are to be seen not as plagiarisms but as homage to the great founder of the epic tradition.

The design of the *Aeneid*

Virgil's basic plan was to link two Golden Ages: that of pre-classical Greece with the one he invented for the Augustan Age. Aeneas of course was one important link in this chain; another was his son, Ascanius, whom Virgil also called Iulus (i.e. Julus). It was a small step from that to suggest that the Julian *gens* (clan or family) traced its origin back to Iulus and so to the goddess Venus. Of course the most famous members of the Julian *gens* were Julius Caesar and his adopted son, Augustus (whose full name following his adoption was Gaius Iulius Caesar Octavianus). In this way Virgil could claim for the emperor a divine origin firmly grounded in the Greek Golden Age.

To overcome the chronological gap between Aeneas and the founding of Rome by Romulus, Virgil decided to make Iulus the first king of a newly-founded city, Alba Longa (situated about 12 miles to the south-east of Rome). There Iulus' descendants would reign as kings until the last in the line, Romulus and Remus, left to found Rome.

The first six books of the *Aeneid* are devoted to the journey of Aeneas and his people westwards from Troy, in search of a new home. They called at various places along the way, often in fact wrongly imagining they had found their promised land; each time prophecies directed them to move on and gave them more clues about their target destination. It is easy to see that this first half of the poem is modelled closely on Homer's *Odyssey*, in which the Greek hero Odysseus, fresh from the capture of Troy, tries to sail home, undergoing numerous adventures along the way.

The second half of the *Aeneid* is set mainly near the estuary of the Tiber, the river that flows through the heart of Rome. Here the Trojans tried to establish a new city for themselves, but fell foul of the local inhabitants, who for various reasons decided to oppose the immigrants. War broke out and this occupies Books VII–XII. Again it is clear that this half was modelled on Homer's *Iliad*, the theme of which is the battles that followed the breakdown of relations between the Greek champion, Achilles, and the commander of the Greek army, Agamemnon, together with the consequences of this rupture.

Early in Book VII, Virgil writes that he is embarking on a *maius opus* – a 'greater work'. In other words, he is signifying that he considers the warfare of Books VII–XII to be a more important theme than the wanderings of the Trojans in Books I–VI. This attitude reflects the view prevalent at the time that heroic combat should be the central theme of the best epic poems. Indeed it is still the view of many that the *Iliad* is a greater work than the *Odyssey*. Today's readers of the *Aeneid*, however, tend to prefer the more varied content of Books I–VI to the more repetitive diet of warfare in Books VII–XII. Nevertheless there are numerous episodes from these later books (including Book XI) that are beautifully written and amply repay the reader's efforts.

The epic form

Homer set the gold standard for epic poetry; poets who followed him made few changes to the form (though some did experiment with the subject matter). From Homer onwards all epics were composed using a particular rhythm or metre, called the dactylic hexameter (see next section: Metre). Although Greek, being more flexible than Latin, was well suited to this rhythm, Roman poets had a more difficult task to match their words to the requirements of the metre. Nevertheless Virgil among others still managed to generate supremely effective and often very beautiful lines of verse.

The standard theme of the epic poem was the actions of heroic figures. Since heroic glory was largely defined by victory in battle, especially in single combat, most of the dominant characters were male, with women relegated to largely domestic roles. The great exceptions to this are (in the Greek epic cycle) tales of the Amazons and their queens; and in Virgil the episode of Camilla in Book XI.

It was always believed that, in the Greek Golden Age, the gods interacted with humans at all levels. Besides success in battle, another determining factor for heroic glory was the extent to which each hero was aided by one or more gods (or conversely overcame hostility from other deities). Thus in the *Aeneid* Aeneas is frequently helped by his mother Venus, while surviving all the attempts of Juno to prevent him from achieving his destiny. In all traditional epic poems, the gods also act out their own personal vendettas against their fellows, so providing a two-tier drama: humans below and the gods above, with periodic interactions between them.

Homer's gods, and to a lesser extent Virgil's, are likened to humans but on a larger, more powerful scale, with similar character flaws and ambitions.

Metre

As stated above, every line of Greek and Roman epic had the same basic rhythm or metre. This metre is called the dactylic hexameter. The word 'dactylic' indicates the nature of the rhythmical unit being used; 'hexameter' tells us that there are six of these units (called 'feet') in each line.

In Latin poetry rhythm is determined by the length of each syllable, either short or long. Scansion involves writing out a line of verse and marking the length of each syllable, by writing above the syllable ∪ if it is short, – if it is long; also the divisions between feet should be marked with a vertical line through the text.

A dactylic hexameter, therefore, consists of six feet, with each foot containing one dactyl (or equivalent). A dactyl consists of one long syllable followed by two short ones, and is marked like this: –∪ ∪. To provide variation of rhythm, each dactyl in the line (apart usually from the fifth one) may be replaced by a spondee, which comprises two long syllables, marked – –. The sixth foot always contains two syllables only, either long + short or long + long. For the purposes of the examination, it is always allowable to mark the final syllable with an *anceps* (x); this is because, with no dictionaries or grammar books allowed, it is sometimes impossible for candidates to know whether this syllable is long or short.

The metrical scheme for a dactylic hexameter therefore looks like this:

$$- - \quad - - \quad - - \quad - - \quad \quad - -$$
$$-\cup\cup| \quad -\cup\cup| \quad -\cup\cup| \quad -\cup\cup| \quad -\cup\cup| \quad -\cup.$$

There are fairly precise rules for determining whether a syllable is short or long. The following are always long:

- diphthongs (in Latin *ae* and *au* are the commonest); also *oe* and, in proper names, *eu* and sometimes *ei*;
- vowels followed by two or more consonants, whether in the same word or the next. An exception to this rule is when the second of two consonants is *l* or *r*, in which case the syllable may be short or long;
- vowels that are long by nature (such as ablative singular endings of the first and second declensions). Where the vowel appears in the stem of a word, dictionaries generally indicate its length.

The following syllables are short:

- single vowels that are followed by a single consonant, or by another vowel that does not form a diphthong, so long as they are normally pronounced as short (dictionaries here too are useful guides).

Scanning a line can be a very useful indicator of which part of a word is being used; for example *puellă* must be nominative or vocative, while *puellā* must be ablative.

Some further rules that need to be mastered are:

- *qu-* and *-gu* before a vowel count as a single consonant (i.e. the *u* is ignored), e.g. *sanguis*;
- *x* and *z* always count as double consonants (and so the vowel before them is always scanned long);
- *i* when followed by another vowel sometimes becomes a consonant (e.g. *iam*, which has one syllable, not two, and *cuius*, which has two syllables); at other times it is treated as a separate vowel (e.g. *audiet, ierat*);
- a vowel at the end of a word elides before a vowel at the start of the next word; when scanning such a line, you should place

brackets round the elided vowel and ignore it when scanning the rest of the line;

- there is one other type of syllable that elides in the same way: any word ending in *-am, -em, -im, -om* or *-um* before a word starting with a vowel should be bracketed and then ignored;
- *h-* at the start of a word should be ignored;
- every dactylic hexameter has a natural pause around the middle; this is known as a caesura (a Latin word with the literal meaning 'cutting'); the caesura is marked by a double vertical line through the line; in most lines the caesura comes after the first syllable of the third foot, as long as it coincides with the end of a word; if that is not possible, the caesura may be placed in the second or fourth foot, again after the first syllable.

It should be noted that the above rules are slightly simplified, but are sufficient for the needs of anyone reading this book. For a more detailed treatment, other sources of information are available (see Further reading).

Let us now put these rules into practice with some examples from Book XI.

$$- \ \cup\cup|- \quad -|- \quad \| \quad -|- \cup \ \cup|- \cup\cup| - \quad -$$
Line 3:   praecipitant curae   turbataque funere mens est

$$- \ \cup\cup|- \cup\cup|- \quad \| \quad -| - \cup\cup| \quad - \cup\cup|- \cup$$
Line 6:   constitu-it tumul-o   fulgentiaqu(e) induit arma

$$- \ \cup\cup| \quad -\cup\cup| \quad - \ \| \ - \ |- \quad -|-\cup\cup|--$$
Line 51:   nos iuven(em) exanim(um) et   nil iam caelestibus ullis

$$- \ \cup\cup|- -| \quad - \cup\cup-| \ \| \quad -|- \ \cup\cup|-\cup$$
Line 56:   vulneribus puls(um) aspici-es,   nec sospite dirum

It can be seen from the above examples that every line is slightly different; in this way variation is introduced. Poets capitalized on this by sometimes making lines strongly dactylic or strongly spondaic.

Dactylic rhythm was considered fast, while spondaic rhythm was thought of as slow. This convention allowed poets to match the rhythm to the subject matter: rapid action or excitement could be emphasized by the abundant use of dactyls, while inactivity, solemnity, sadness or awe could be enhanced by the use of spondees. An example of the former is line 22:

$$- \cup\cup\,|- \cup\cup\,|- \,\|\cup\ \cup\,|- \cup\cup\,|- \ \cup\cup\,|- \ -$$

intere-a soci- os   inhumataque corpora terrae

Here Aeneas is urging his men to hurry; the rhythm is the fastest possible, to underscore the haste. An example of the latter is line 27:

$$- \ -|- \ -|- \,\| \qquad - \ | - \ - \,|- \cup\cup\,|- \ \cup$$

mittatur Pallas,   quem non virtutis eg-entem

Here Aeneas gives orders for the body of the young hero Pallas to be returned to his grieving city; the rhythm is the slowest possible, to emphasize the sadness of Aeneas and his men at their loss.

Further variation was achieved by the competition between the metrical stress (called the ictus), always on the first syllable of each foot, and the natural stress of each word. Sometimes the two stresses are synchronized on the same syllable throughout the line, giving a smooth rhythm; at other times they fall on different syllables, giving a jerkier rhythm. It should be noted that the level of analysis required to inform meaningful discussion of this interplay of stresses is generally considered outside the scope of the A-Level specification; there is nothing, however, to prevent any student from including such discussion in an examination response if so desired. Scansion itself requires no knowledge of it.

Virgil's style

In the context of poetry, style is a difficult word to define. It encapsulates all the features of language that a poet has incorporated into his work.

From Homer onwards (and probably even earlier), stylistic features were continually invented, refined and adopted into the palette of techniques that each poet wielded. Some of these techniques were common to both poetry and prose; others helped to define poetry and to distinguish it from prose.

Examination questions often use the formula 'You should refer to both what the poet says and how he says it' (or similar). This is the standard instruction to candidates to embrace both content and style in their analysis of a passage. 'What the poet says' is the basic plot or storyline; of itself, it may be interesting and even entertaining, but it is not yet poetry. It is the 'how he says it' that turns the prosaic into poetry.

The most obvious technique that distinguishes poetry from prose is the rhythm, as described above. Another is the use of so-called 'poetic' vocabulary, comprising words that prose writers would not normally use. A further technique, also found in some prose writing, is the use of imagery; this may be on the small scale, for example the use of a metaphorical word or phrase; on the medium scale through the use of an extended or epic simile; or on the large scale in the form of allegory (a kind of extended metaphor often worked up into a complete storyline). All of these involve the creation of a word-picture that stimulates the imagination of the reader, in the same way that a good artist uses colours, textures, symbols and shapes to create a complex image that may delight or shock the observer.

A general feature of Latin verse is that key words tend to be placed at the beginning or end of a line. This is not always the case, but a rapid perusal of a few lines will show how frequent this ordering of words is. This can often help us to understand what feature of a line was considered most important by the poet.

In addition to these broad techniques, Virgil had an arsenal of stylistic devices at his disposal, each one used to add subtle hues to the colours of the word-picture he was creating. One of the principal reasons why it is more rewarding to read the *Aeneid* in the original Latin than in a translation is that many of the stylistic devices inevitably disappear in translation, and the perceived quality of the poetry suffers as a result. Also translators cannot avoid adding colour of their own: compare any two or three translations published over the past century or so and you will see that they differ widely in style and language.

As a reader of the *Aeneid*, the more familiar you are with Virgil's stylistic devices, the more rewarding you will find your experience. As an examination candidate, you will be asked to analyse a few lines of the poem, in order to demonstrate how the poet's use of a range of devices makes the poetry more effective. For these reasons a list of stylistic devices (not exhaustive but sufficient for our purposes) is provided below, each with one or more examples from the text. A worked example and guidance on how to structure such an analysis can be found on the companion website to this book.

In the Commentary following the text, no attempt will be made to identify every instance of a stylistic device; to do so would double the size of the book. Generally only the most significant examples will merit a comment. Readers should aim to familiarize themselves with the commonest devices sufficiently thoroughly to enable them both to recognize them when they encounter them as they read, and to evaluate their impact. This is far preferable to trying to memorize every individual occurrence.

At all costs, readers should avoid treating stylistic analysis as a sterile cataloguing of devices: to be told that there is a chiasmus in line so-and-so tells us nothing about the poetic quality of the line. It is much more useful to consider *why* Virgil might have chosen to include this feature and what effect it has on your understanding and appreciation.

Catalogue of stylistic devices

alliteration: a sound effect created by the grouping of two or more words with the same initial consonant. The intention may be no more than to draw attention to particular words or to link them in readers' minds; certain letters however are frequently used to suggest particular emotions. See also **consonance**, where the repetition is of consonants inside words. Examples are:

- *f-, s-* regularly represent a hissing sound, whether relating to snakes or reflecting anger, bitterness or horror (note that repeated *-s-* sounds are sometimes called **sibilance**):

    - *inferias, caeso sparsurus sanguine flammas* (82)
      '[men whom he would send to the underworld] as offerings, intending to spatter the flames [of the pyre] with shed blood'

- *l-, m-* frequently represent the calm of sleep or death:

    - *labitur exsanguis, labuntur frigida leto / lumina* (818–19)
      '[Camilla] sank down after losing blood, [and] her eyes, cold in death, began to droop'

- *m-* also regularly represents anger or grieving:

    - *primitiae manibusque meis Mezentius hic est* (16)
      '[these are] the first spoils of war [from an arrogant king] and here is Mezentius, killed by my hands' (anger)
    - *cum me complexus euntem / mitteret in magnum imperium metuensque moneret* (46–7)
      'when having embraced me as I left he sent me to (win) a great empire and he fearfully warned ...' (grief)

- *p-* often reflects bitterness or contempt:

    - *hanc patriam peperere suo, decorate supremis* (25)

'adorn with final [offerings the splendid spirits who] won this homeland with their [blood]' (bitterness)

anaphora: the repetition of the same word to introduce two or more parallel statements, the intention being to emphasize those words:

- *ter circum accensos cincti fulgentibus armis*
  decurrere rogos, ter maestum funeris ignem / lustravere (188–90)
  'three times they processed round the burning pyres, clad in their shining armour, three times they circled the sad fire of death'

antithesis: two words of opposite meaning are placed together to heighten the contrast:

- *solacia luctus exigua ingentis* (62–3)
  'a very small consolation for a very great grief'

apostrophe: a direct appeal by the poet to a god, person or place that is not present in the narrative:

- *fulgentiaque induit arma, / Mezenti ducis exuvias, tibi, magne,*
  tropaeum, / bellipotens (6–8)
  'and he dressed [the trunk of a tree] with the shining armour,
  the spoils of the chieftain Mezentius, as a trophy to you,
  great War-god'

assonance: the repetition of vowel sounds in nearby words (both at the beginning and in the middle). This device is similar to **alliteration**. Three vowels when repeated tend to have certain effects:

- *-a-* regularly reflects high emotion, particularly sadness and anger:

  - *arma parate animis . . .* (18)
    'prepare for war in your hearts'

- *-o-* expresses surprise or admiration:

○ *telum ... quod forte gerebat / bellator, solidum nodis et robore cocto* (552–3)
  'the javelin ... which by chance the warrior was carrying, tough with knots and fire-hardened oak'

• -*u*- expresses grief:

○ *ter maestum funeris ignem / lustravere in equis ululatusque ore dedere* (189–90)
  'three times they circled the sad fire of death on their horses and they uttered howls of grief from their mouths'

asyndeton: the lack of conjunctions to join parallel words, phrases or clauses (the opposite is **polysyndeton**). The effect is often to speed up a sequence of events:

• *sonuere undae, rapidum super amnem / infelix fugit ... Camilla* (562–3)
  'the waters resounded, Camilla flew unfortunate over the rapid river'

chiasmus: two parallel phrases, the second of which is in reverse order to the first. This is originally a rhetorical device, used to add elegance and force to an argument:

• *arma parate animis et spe praesumite bellum* (18)
  'for conflict prepare in your hearts and with hope look forward to war'

consonance: the repetition of a consonant within neighbouring words. This is similar to **alliteration**, and is usually used in conjunction with it:

• see 25 and 82 above, under **alliteration**.

enclosing word-order: a phrase in which two or more words relating to one object, action or state enclose one or more words relating to a second object, action or state, in such a way that they reflect the sense of the phrase. For example *in medio stat foro* has the verb enclosed within *in medio foro*, reflecting what is actually happening. (NB: the term is used here more narrowly than some other editors do, who use it to define any pair of words that enclose others.)

- *maestoque immugit regia luctu* (38)
  'and the king's home resounded with sad lamentation' (the sad lamentation surrounds the king's home, emphasizing the amount of lamentation)

enjambment: the carrying over of sense to the beginning of the next line. The effect is to place extra emphasis on the word that is carried over:

- *pacem me exanimis et Martis sorte peremptis / oratis?* (110–11)
  'are you (really) asking me for a truce for [burying] the dead and those killed by the lottery of War?'

hendiadys: the separation of an adjective-plus-noun phrase into two parallel nouns linked by a conjunction. It is used to give greater emphasis to the words:

- *haud segnes alii crates et molle feretrum* (64)
  'not slowly did others (prepare) wicker-work and a soft bier' (i.e. a bier of soft wicker-work)

hypallage or **transferred epithet:** the transfer of an adjective from the noun to which it logically belongs to another noun in the same phrase:

- *et maestum Iliades crinem de more solutae* (35)
  'and the women of Troy having let down their sad hair according to custom' (logically it is the women who are sad)

hyperbaton: the separation of words that belong syntactically together by intervening words that are not part of the same phrase. This is so common in poetry that it rarely deserves special comment:

- *vota deum* **primo** *victor solvebat* **Eoo** (4)
  'the victor fulfilled his vows to the gods at first light'

hyperbole: this is simply a synonym for exaggeration, obviously to emphasize a point:

- *ingentem gemitum tunsis ad sidera tollunt / pectoribus* (37–8)
  'beating their breasts they raised a huge groan to the stars'

litotes: a form of understatement that uses a negative, often a double negative, to give more emphasis than a positive expression, like the English 'not bad', which usually means 'very good':

- *haud segnes alii crates et molle feretrum* (64)
  'not slowly did others (prepare) wicker-work and a soft bier'

metaphor: the use of a word with a meaning different from its literal or normal one. Whereas a simile says that one thing is *like* another (e.g. 'the world is like a stage'), a metaphor says one thing *is* another (e.g. 'the world is a stage'):

- *at medias inter caedes exsultat Amazon* (648)
  'but in the midst of the slaughter the Amazon [i.e. Camilla] runs amok'

metonymy: calling something not by its own name but by the name of something related to it:

- *pacem me exanimis et Martis sorte peremptis / oratis?* (110–11)
  'are you (really) asking me for a truce for [burying] the dead and those killed by the lottery of Mars?' (the name of the god of War is substituted for actual war)

onomatopoeia: a word that sounds like what it means:

- *lustravere in equis ululatusque ore dedere* (190)
  'they circled on their horses and they uttered howls of grief from their mouths'

oxymoron: the juxtaposition of two words of opposing or contradictory meaning:

- *subito vix* (551)
  'suddenly reluctantly'

polyptoton: the repetition of a noun, verb or pronoun with different endings (closely related to **anaphora**):

- *spargitur et tellus lacrimis, sparguntur et arma* (191)
  'both the earth is spattered with tears, and their arms are spattered'

polysyndeton: the repeated use of conjunctions (usually 'and') in quick succession to join words or phrases; sometimes more are used than necessary. The effect may be to give a sense of rapidity to a sequence, or it may stress the number of items in the sequence:

- *vestes auroque ostroque rigentes* (72)
  'garments stiff with gold and purple'

prolepsis: the anticipation of a future act or state by treating it as if it already existed:

- *ultricem pharetra deprome sagittam* (590)
  'take an avenging arrow from the quiver' (the arrow has not yet avenged Camilla's death)

rhetorical question: a question (often in a series) asked, not to elicit a reply, but as a stronger alternative to a statement:

- *hi nostri reditus exspectatique triumphi? / haec mea magna fides?* (54–5)

'Is this the return and the triumphs we were expecting? Is this my great trust?'

sibilance: see under **alliteration.**

simile: a comparison of one thing, event or scene with another one. A simple simile is generally introduced by the prepositional 'like' or 'as'. Like Homer, Virgil most often uses extended or 'epic' similes, often several lines long; they are introduced by some part of *qualis* (68–71; 659–63) or *ut cum* (751–6, where the following *haud aliter*, meaning 'in just the same way', relates the simile to the narrative episode) or *velut* (809–13, followed by *haud secus*).

synchysis: an interlocking of the word order of two pairs of words, so that the words that belong syntactically together are separated. For example the order may be adjective – noun – adjective – noun, where the first adjective defines the second noun; or it may be adjective – adjective – noun – noun (this variety, with the verb in the middle, is known as a 'golden line'):

- *cetera confusaeque ingentem caedis acervum* (207)
  '[they cremated] the rest, a huge pile of chaotic carnage'

synecdoche: the substitution of a part of something for the whole thing:

- *qui solus honos Acheronte sub imo est* (23)
  'which is the only honour down in the deepest Acheron' (i.e. the Underworld)

tricolon: a series of three parallel expressions, used mainly by orators to give extra force to an argument. (Occasionally four parallel expressions are linked to form a **tetracolon.**) To give even greater force, the three expressions may increase in length; this is called a **tricolon crescens:**

- *o fama ingens, ingentior armis, vir Troiane* (124–5)

  'O (man) great of reputation, (man) greater in arms, Trojan man'

zeugma: the use of one verb with two objects, requiring the verb to bear a different meaning with each object:

- *hos aditus iamque hos aditus omnemque pererrat / undique circuitum* (766–7)

  'he **tries** now this approach and now that, and **wanders through** a whole circuit all round'

Further reading

There have been several translations produced in the Penguin Classics Series, of which my favourite is by W. F. Jackson Knight; more recent ones are by David West and Robert Fagles. All have their individual approach to the art of translation, and none can transmit the full scope of Virgil's genius.

Editions consulted in preparing this text are those by T. E. Page, Macmillan, 1900 and 1962 (Books VII–XII); R. D. Williams, BCP, 1973 and 1996 (Books VII–XII); and K. W. Gransden, CUP, 1991 (Book XI).

More general books are K. Quinn *Virgil's Aeneid*, Routledge & Kegan Paul, 1968, and W. A. Camps *An Introduction to Virgil*, OUP, 1969.

For the metre, see S. E. Winbolt, *The Latin Hexameter*, Blackie and Son Limited, 1906; and D. S. Raven, *Latin Metre: an Introduction*, Faber and Faber, 1965.

Text

Oceanum interea surgens Aurora reliquit:
Aeneas, quamquam et sociis dare tempus humandis
praecipitant curae turbataque funere mens est,
vota deum primo victor solvebat Eoo.
ingentem quercum decisis undique ramis 5
constituit tumulo fulgentiaque induit arma,
Mezenti ducis exuvias, tibi, magne, tropaeum,
bellipotens; aptat rorantes sanguine cristas
telaque trunca viri, et bis sex thoraca petitum
perfossumque locis, clipeumque ex aere sinistrae 10
subligat atque ensem collo suspendit eburnum.
tum socios (namque omnis eum stipata tegebat
turba ducum) sic incipiens hortatur ovantes:
'maxima res effecta, viri; timor omnis abesto,
quod superest; haec sunt spolia et de rege superbo 15
primitiae manibusque meis Mezentius hic est.
nunc iter ad regem nobis murosque Latinos.
arma parate animis et spe praesumite bellum,
ne qua mora ignaros, ubi primum vellere signa
adnuerint superi pubemque educere castris, 20
impediat segnisve metu sententia tardet.
interea socios inhumataque corpora terrae
mandemus, qui solus honos Acheronte sub imo est.
ite' ait, 'egregias animas, quae sanguine nobis
hanc patriam peperere suo, decorate supremis 25
muneribus, maestamque Euandri primus ad urbem
mittatur Pallas, quem non virtutis egentem
abstulit atra dies et funere mersit acerbo.'
    sic ait inlacrimans, recipitque ad limina gressum
corpus ubi exanimi positum Pallantis Acoetes 30
servabat senior, qui Parrhasio Euandro

armiger ante fuit, sed non felicibus aeque
tum comes auspiciis caro datus ibat alumno.
circum omnis famulumque manus Troianaque turba
et maestum Iliades crinem de more solutae.   35
ut vero Aeneas foribus sese intulit altis
ingentem gemitum tunsis ad sidera tollunt
pectoribus, maestoque immugit regia luctu.
ipse caput nivei fultum Pallantis et ora
ut vidit levique patens in pectore vulnus   40
cuspidis Ausoniae, lacrimis ita fatur obortis:
'tene' inquit, 'miserande puer, cum laeta veniret,
invidit Fortuna mihi, ne regna videres
nostra neque ad sedes victor veherere paternas?
non haec Euandro de te promissa parenti   45
discedens dederam, cum me complexus euntem
mitteret in magnum imperium metuensque moneret
acres esse viros, cum dura proelia gente.
et nunc ille quidem spe multum captus inani
fors et vota facit cumulatque altaria donis,   50
nos iuvenem exanimum et nil iam caelestibus ullis
debentem vano maesti comitamur honore.
infelix, nati funus crudele videbis!
hi nostri reditus exspectatique triumphi?
haec mea magna fides? at non, Euandre, pudendis   55
vulneribus pulsum aspicies, nec sospite dirum
optabis nato funus pater. hei mihi, quantum
praesidium, Ausonia, et quantum tu perdis, Iule!'
    haec ubi deflevit, tolli miserabile corpus
imperat, et toto lectos ex agmine mittit   60
mille viros qui supremum comitentur honorem
intersintque patris lacrimis, solacia luctus
exigua ingentis, misero sed debita patri.
haud segnes alii crates et molle feretrum
arbuteis texunt virgis et vimine querno   65
exstructosque toros obtentu frondis inumbrant.

AS

hic iuvenem agresti sublimem stramine ponunt:
qualem virgineo demessum pollice florem
seu mollis violae seu languentis hyacinthi,
cui neque fulgor adhuc nec dum sua forma recessit, 70
non iam mater alit tellus viresque ministrat.
tum geminas vestes auroque ostroque rigentes
extulit Aeneas, quas illi laeta laborum
ipsa suis quondam manibus Sidonia Dido
fecerat et tenui telas discreverat auro. 75
harum unam iuveni supremum maestus honorem
induit arsurasque comas obnubit amictu,
multaque praeterea Laurentis praemia pugnae
aggerat et longo praedam iubet ordine duci;
addit equos et tela quibus spoliaverat hostem. 80
vinxerat et post terga manus, quos mitteret umbris
inferias, caeso sparsurus sanguine flammas,
indutosque iubet truncos hostilibus armis
ipsos ferre duces inimicaque nomina figi.
ducitur infelix aevo confectus Acoetes, 85
pectora nunc foedans pugnis, nunc unguibus ora,
sternitur et toto proiectus corpore terrae.
ducunt et Rutulo perfusos sanguine currus.
post bellator equus positis insignibus Aethon
it lacrimans guttisque umectat grandibus ora. 90
hastam alii galeamque ferunt, nam cetera Turnus
victor habet. tum maesta phalanx Teucrique sequuntur
Tyrrhenique omnes et versis Arcades armis.
postquam omnis longe comitum praecesserat ordo,
substitit Aeneas gemituque haec addidit alto: 95
'nos alias hinc ad lacrimas eadem horrida belli
fata vocant: salve aeternum mihi, maxime Palla,
aeternumque vale.' nec plura effatus ad altos
tendebat muros gressumque in castra ferebat.
    iamque oratores aderant ex urbe Latina 100
velati ramis oleae veniamque rogantes:

A S

corpora, per campos ferro quae fusa iacebant,
redderet ac tumulo sineret succedere terrae:
nullum cum victis certamen et aethere cassis;
parceret hospitibus quondam socerisque vocatis.   105
quos bonus Aeneas haud aspernanda precantes
prosequitur venia et verbis haec insuper addit:
'quaenam vos tanto fortuna indigna, Latini,
implicuit bello, qui nos fugiatis amicos?
pacem me exanimis et Martis sorte peremptis   110
oratis? equidem et vivis concedere vellem.
nec veni, nisi fata locum sedemque dedissent,
nec bellum cum gente gero; rex nostra reliquit
hospitia et Turni potius se credidit armis.
aequius huic Turnum fuerat se opponere morti.   115
si bellum finire manu, si pellere Teucros
apparat, his mecum decuit concurrere telis:
vixet cui vitam deus aut sua dextra dedisset.
nunc ite et miseris supponite civibus ignem.'
dixerat Aeneas. illi obstipuere silentes   120
conversique oculos inter se atque ora tenebant.
    tum senior semperque odiis et crimine Drances
infensus iuveni Turno sic ore vicissim
orsa refert: 'o fama ingens, ingentior armis,
vir Troiane, quibus caelo te laudibus aequem?   125
iustitiaene prius mirer belline laborum?
nos vero haec patriam grati referemus ad urbem
et te, si qua viam dederit fortuna, Latino
iungemus regi. quaerat sibi foedera Turnus.
quin et fatales murorum attollere moles   130
saxaque subvectare umeris Troiana iuvabit.'
dixerat haec unoque omnes eadem ore fremebant.
bis senos pepigere dies, et pace sequestra
per silvas Teucri mixtique impune Latini
erravere iugis. ferro sonat alta bipenni   135
fraxinus, evertunt actas ad sidera pinus,

robora nec cuneis et olentem scindere cedrum
nec plaustris cessant vectare gementibus ornos.
    et iam Fama volans, tanti praenuntia luctus,
Euandrum Euandrique domos et moenia replet,   140
quae modo victorem Latio Pallanta ferebat.
Arcades ad portas ruere et de more vetusto
funereas rapuere faces; lucet via longo
ordine flammarum et late discriminat agros.
contra turba Phrygum veniens plangentia iungit   145
agmina. quae postquam matres succedere tectis
viderunt, maestam incendunt clamoribus urbem.
at non Euandrum potis est vis ulla tenere,
sed venit in medios. feretro Pallanta reposto
procubuit super atque haeret lacrimansque gemensque,   150
et via vix tandem voci laxata dolore est:
'non haec, o Palla, dederas promissa petenti,
cautius ut saevo velles te credere Marti.
haud ignarus eram quantum nova gloria in armis
et praedulce decus primo certamine posset.   155
primitiae iuvenis miserae bellique propinqui
dura rudimenta, et nulli exaudita deorum
vota precesque meae! tuque, o sanctissima coniunx,
felix morte tua neque in hunc servata dolorem!
contra ego vivendo vici mea fata, superstes   160
restarem ut genitor. Troum socia arma secutum
obruerent Rutuli telis! animam ipse dedissem
atque haec pompa domum me, non Pallanta, referret!
nec vos arguerim, Teucri, nec foedera nec quas
iunximus hospitio dextras: sors ista senectae   165
debita erat nostrae. quod si immatura manebat
mors natum, caesis Volscorum milibus ante
ducentem in Latium Teucros cecidisse iuvabit.
quin ego non alio digner te funere, Palla,
quam pius Aeneas et quam magni Phryges et quam   170
Tyrrhenique duces, Tyrrhenum exercitus omnis.

AS

magna tropaea ferunt quos dat tua dextera leto;
tu quoque nunc stares immanis truncus in armis,
esset par aetas et idem si robur ab annis,
Turne. sed infelix Teucros quid demoror armis?   175
vadite et haec memores regi mandata referte:
quod vitam moror invisam Pallante perempto
dextera causa tua est, Turnum natoque patrique
quam debere vides. meritis vacat hic tibi solus
fortunaeque locus. non vitae gaudia quaero,   180
nec fas, sed nato manes perferre sub imos.'
   Aurora interea miseris mortalibus almam
extulerat lucem referens opera atque labores:
iam pater Aeneas, iam curvo in litore Tarchon
constituere pyras. huc corpora quisque suorum   185
more tulere patrum, subiectisque ignibus atris
conditur in tenebras altum caligine caelum.
ter circum accensos cincti fulgentibus armis
decurrere rogos, ter maestum funeris ignem
lustravere in equis ululatusque ore dedere.   190
spargitur et tellus lacrimis, sparguntur et arma,
it caelo clamorque virum clangorque tubarum.
hic alii spolia occisis derepta Latinis
coniciunt igni, galeas ensesque decoros
frenaque ferventesque rotas; pars munera nota,   195
ipsorum clipeos et non felicia tela.
multa boum circa mactantur corpora Morti,
saetigerosque sues raptasque ex omnibus agris
in flammam iugulant pecudes. tum litore toto
ardentes spectant socios semustaque servant   200
busta, neque avelli possunt, nox umida donec
invertit caelum stellis ardentibus aptum.
   nec minus et miseri diversa in parte Latini
innumeras struxere pyras, et corpora partim
multa virum terrae infodiunt, avectaque partim   205
finitimos tollunt in agros urbique remittunt.

cetera confusaeque ingentem caedis acervum
nec numero nec honore cremant; tunc undique vasti
certatim crebris conlucent ignibus agri.
tertia lux gelidam caelo dimoverat umbram: 210
maerentes altum cinerem et confusa ruebant
ossa focis tepidoque onerabant aggere terrae.
iam vero in tectis, praedivitis urbe Latini,
praecipuus fragor et longi pars maxima luctus.
hic matres miseraeque nurus, hic cara sororum   215
pectora maerentum puerique parentibus orbi
dirum exsecrantur bellum Turnique hymenaeos;
ipsum armis ipsumque iubent decernere ferro,
qui regnum Italiae et primos sibi poscat honores.
ingravat haec saevus Drances solumque vocari   220
testatur, solum posci in certamina Turnum.
multa simul contra variis sententia dictis
pro Turno, et magnum reginae nomen obumbrat,
multa virum meritis sustentat fama tropaeis.

*225–497: The Latins learn that they have failed to win the help of
Diomede, one of the Greek leaders in the Trojan War, who has settled in
Italy. Latinus recommends at a council of war that they offer peace to
the Trojans; he is supported by Drances but opposed by Turnus. As they
are debating, guards report that the Trojans are about to attack the city.
Turnus takes charge of the defences.*

   obvia cui Volscorum acie comitante Camilla
occurrit portisque ab equo regina sub ipsis
desiluit, quam tota cohors imitata relictis   500
ad terram defluxit equis; tum talia fatur:
'Turne, sui merito si qua est fiducia forti,
audeo et Aeneadum promitto occurrere turmae
solaque Tyrrhenos equites ire obvia contra.
me sine prima manu temptare pericula belli,   505
tu pedes ad muros subsiste et moenia serva.'
Turnus ad haec oculos horrenda in virgine fixus:
'o decus Italiae virgo, quas dicere grates
quasve referre parem? sed nunc, est omnia quando
iste animus supra, mecum partire laborem.   510
Aeneas, ut fama fidem missique reportant
exploratores, equitum levia improbus arma
praemisit, quaterent campos; ipse ardua montis
per deserta iugo superans adventat ad urbem.
furta paro belli convexo in tramite silvae,   515
ut bivias armato obsidam milite fauces.
tu Tyrrhenum equitem conlatis excipe signis;
tecum acer Messapus erit turmaeque Latinae
Tiburtique manus, ducis et tu concipe curam.'
sic ait, et paribus Messapum in proelia dictis   520
hortatur sociosque duces et pergit in hostem.

**A
Level**

522–31: Turnus sets up an ambush at the head of a valley that the Trojans must pass through on their way to Laurentum.

velocem interea superis in sedibus Opim,
unam ex virginibus sociis sacraque caterva,
compellabat et has tristes Latonia voces
ore dabat: 'graditur bellum ad crudele Camilla,   535
o virgo, et nostris nequiquam cingitur armis,
cara mihi ante alias. neque enim novus iste Dianae
venit amor subitaque animum dulcedine movit.
pulsus ob invidiam regno viresque superbas
Priverno antiqua Metabus cum excederet urbe,   540
infantem fugiens media inter proelia belli
sustulit exsilio comitem, matrisque vocavit
nomine Casmillae mutata parte Camillam.
ipse sinu prae se portans iuga longa petebat
solorum nemorum: tela undique saeva premebant   545
et circumfuso volitabant milite Volsci.
ecce fugae medio summis Amasenus abundans
spumabat ripis, tantus se nubibus imber
ruperat. ille innare parans infantis amore
tardatur caroque oneri timet. omnia secum   550
versanti subito vix haec sententia sedit:
telum immane manu valida quod forte gerebat
bellator, solidum nodis et robore cocto,
huic natam libro et silvestri subere clausam
implicat atque habilem mediae circumligat hastae;   555
quam dextra ingenti librans ita ad aethera fatur:
"alma, tibi hanc, nemorum cultrix, Latonia virgo,
ipse pater famulam voveo; tua prima per auras
tela tenens supplex hostem fugit. accipe, testor,
diva tuam, quae nunc dubiis committitur auris."   560
dixit, et adducto contortum hastile lacerto
immittit: sonuere undae, rapidum super amnem
infelix fugit in iaculo stridente Camilla.

A Level

at Metabus magna propius iam urgente caterva
dat sese fluvio, atque hastam cum virgine victor   565
gramineo, donum Triviae, de caespite vellit.
non illum tectis ullae, non moenibus urbes
accepere (neque ipse manus feritate dedisset),
pastorum et solis exegit montibus aevum.
hic natam in dumis interque horrentia lustra   570
armentalis equae mammis et lacte ferino
nutribat teneris immulgens ubera labris.
utque pedum primis infans vestigia plantis
institerat, iaculo palmas armavit acuto
spiculaque ex umero parvae suspendit et arcum.   575
pro crinali auro, pro longae tegmine pallae
tigridis exuviae per dorsum a vertice pendent.
tela manu iam tum tenera puerilia torsit
et fundam tereti circum caput egit habena
Strymoniamque gruem aut album deiecit olorem.   580
multae illam frustra Tyrrhena per oppida matres
optavere nurum; sola contenta Diana
aeternum telorum et virginitatis amorem
intemerata colit. vellem haud correpta fuisset
militia tali conata lacessere Teucros: 585
cara mihi comitumque foret nunc una mearum.
verum age, quandoquidem fatis urgetur acerbis,
labere, nympha, polo finesque invise Latinos,
tristis ubi infausto committitur omine pugna.
haec cape et ultricem pharetra deprome sagittam: 590
hac, quicumque sacrum violarit vulnere corpus,
Tros Italusque, mihi pariter det sanguine poenas.
post ego nube cava miserandae corpus et arma
inspoliata feram tumulo patriaeque reponam.'
dixit, at illa leves caeli delapsa per auras   595
insonuit nigro circumdata turbine corpus.

A
Level

597–647: The cavalry of the Trojans and their allies approach Laurentum. The Latins and their allies ride to meet them. The battle ebbs and flows, with first one side and then the other achieving dominance. Finally, the two sides become locked together in combat, with neither side giving way.

at medias inter caedes exsultat Amazon
unum exserta latus pugnae, pharetrata Camilla,
et nunc lenta manu spargens hastilia denset,   650
nunc validam dextra rapit indefessa bipennem;
aureus ex umero sonat arcus et arma Dianae.
illa etiam, si quando in tergum pulsa recessit,
spicula converso fugientia derigit arcu.
at circum lectae comites, Larinaque virgo   655
Tullaque et aeratam quatiens Tarpeia securim,
Italides, quas ipsa decus sibi dia Camilla
delegit pacisque bonas bellique ministras:
quales Threiciae cum flumina Thermodontis
pulsant et pictis bellantur Amazones armis,   660
seu circum Hippolyten seu cum se Martia curru
Penthesilea refert, magnoque ululante tumultu
feminea exsultant lunatis agmina peltis.
    quem telo primum, quem postremum, aspera virgo,
deicis? aut quot humi morientia corpora fundis?   665
Eunaeum Clytio primum patre, cuius apertum
adversi longa transverberat abiete pectus.
sanguinis ille vomens rivos cadit atque cruentam
mandit humum moriensque suo se in vulnere versat.
tum Lirim Pagasumque super, quorum alter habenas   670
suffuso revolutus equo dum colligit, alter
dum subit ac dextram labenti tendit inermem,
praecipites pariterque ruunt. his addit Amastrum
Hippotaden, sequiturque incumbens eminus hasta
Tereaque Harpalycumque et Demophoonta Chromimque;   675
quotque emissa manu contorsit spicula virgo,
tot Phrygii cecidere viri. procul Ornytus armis

A
Level

ignotis et equo venator Iapyge fertur,
cui pellis latos umeros erepta iuvenco
pugnatori operit, caput ingens oris hiatus   680
et malae texere lupi cum dentibus albis,
agrestisque manus armat sparus; ipse catervis
vertitur in mediis et toto vertice supra est.
hunc illa exceptum (neque enim labor agmine verso)
traicit et super haec inimico pectore fatur: 685
'silvis te, Tyrrhene, feras agitare putasti?
advenit qui vestra dies muliebribus armis
verba redargueret. nomen tamen haud leve patrum
manibus hoc referes, telo cecidisse Camillae.'

*690–724: Camilla continues her killing spree, even chasing after one
fleeing man on foot and killing him.*

   at non haec nullis hominum sator atque deorum   725
observans oculis summo sedet altus Olympo.
Tyrrhenum genitor Tarchonem in proelia saeva
suscitat et stimulis haud mollibus inicit iras.
ergo inter caedes cedentiaque agmina Tarchon
fertur equo variisque instigat vocibus alas   730
nomine quemque vocans, reficitque in proelia pulsos.
'quis metus, o numquam dolituri, o semper inertes
Tyrrheni, quae tanta animis ignavia venit?
femina palantes agit atque haec agmina vertit!
quo ferrum quidve haec gerimus tela inrita dextris?   735
at non in Venerem segnes nocturnaque bella,
aut ubi curva choros indixit tibia Bacchi.
exspectate dapes et plenae pocula mensae
(hic amor, hoc studium) dum sacra secundus haruspex
nuntiet ac lucos vocet hostia pinguis in altos!'   740
haec effatus equum in medios moriturus et ipse
concitat, et Venulo adversum se turbidus infert
dereptumque ab equo dextra complectitur hostem

**A
Level**

et gremium ante suum multa vi concitus aufert.
tollitur in caelum clamor cunctique Latini   745
convertere oculos. volat igneus aequore Tarchon
arma virumque ferens; tum summa ipsius ab hasta
defringit ferrum et partes rimatur apertas,
qua vulnus letale ferat; contra ille repugnans
sustinet a iugulo dextram et vim viribus exit.   750
utque volans alte raptum cum fulva draconem
fert aquila implicuitque pedes atque unguibus haesit,
saucius at serpens sinuosa volumina versat
arrectisque horret squamis et sibilat ore
arduus insurgens, illa haud minus urget obunco   755
luctantem rostro, simul aethera verberat alis:
haud aliter praedam Tiburtum ex agmine Tarchon
portat ovans. ducis exemplum eventumque secuti
Maeonidae incurrunt. tum fatis debitus Arruns
velocem iaculo et multa prior arte Camillam   760
circuit, et quae sit fortuna facillima temptat.
qua se cumque furens medio tulit agmine virgo,
hac Arruns subit et tacitus vestigia lustrat;
qua victrix redit illa pedemque ex hoste reportat,
hac iuvenis furtim celeres detorquet habenas.   765
hos aditus iamque hos aditus omnemque pererrat
undique circuitum et certam quatit improbus hastam.
    forte sacer Cybelo Chloreus olimque sacerdos
insignis longe Phrygiis fulgebat in armis
spumantemque agitabat equum, quem pellis aënis   770
in plumam squamis auro conserta tegebat.
ipse peregrina ferrugine clarus et ostro
spicula torquebat Lycio Gortynia cornu;
aureus ex umeris erat arcus et aurea vati
cassida; tum croceam chlamydemque sinusque crepantes   775
carbaseos fulvo in nodum collegerat auro,
pictus acu tunicas et barbara tegmina crurum.
hunc virgo, sive ut templis praefigeret arma

A
Level

Troia, captivo sive ut se ferret in auro
venatrix, unum ex omni certamine pugnae 780
caeca sequebatur totumque incauta per agmen
femineo praedae et spoliorum ardebat amore,
telum ex insidiis cum tandem tempore capto
concitat et superos Arruns sic voce precatur:
'summe deum, sancti custos Soractis Apollo, 785
quem primi colimus, cui pineus ardor acervo
pascitur, et medium freti pietate per ignem
cultores multa premimus vestigia pruna,
da, pater, hoc nostris aboleri dedecus armis,
omnipotens. non exuvias pulsaeve tropaeum 790
virginis aut spolia ulla peto, mihi cetera laudem
facta ferent; haec dira meo dum vulnere pestis
pulsa cadat, patrias remeabo inglorius urbes.'
    audiit et voti Phoebus succedere partem
mente dedit, partem volucres dispersit in auras: 795
sterneret ut subita turbatam morte Camillam
adnuit oranti; reducem ut patria alta videret
non dedit, inque Notos vocem vertere procellae.
ergo ut missa manu sonitum dedit hasta per auras,
convertere animos acres oculosque tulere 800
cuncti ad reginam Volsci. nihil ipsa nec aurae
nec sonitus memor aut venientis ab aethere teli,
hasta sub exsertam donec perlata papillam
haesit virgineumque alte bibit acta cruorem.
concurrunt trepidae comites dominamque ruentem 805
suscipiunt. fugit ante omnes exterritus Arruns
laetitia mixtoque metu, nec iam amplius hastae
credere nec telis occurrere virginis audet.
ac velut ille, prius quam tela inimica sequantur,
continuo in montes sese avius abdidit altos 810
occiso pastore lupus magnove iuvenco,
conscius audacis facti, caudamque remulcens
subiecit pavitantem utero silvasque petivit:

A Level

haud secus ex oculis se turbidus abstulit Arruns
contentusque fuga mediis se immiscuit armis.   815
illa manu moriens telum trahit, ossa sed inter
ferreus ad costas alto stat vulnere mucro.
labitur exsanguis, labuntur frigida leto
lumina, purpureus quondam color ora reliquit.
tum sic exspirans Accam ex aequalibus unam   820
adloquitur, fida ante alias quae sola Camillae
quicum partiri curas, atque haec ita fatur:
'hactenus, Acca soror, potui: nunc vulnus acerbum
conficit, et tenebris nigrescunt omnia circum.
effuge et haec Turno mandata novissima perfer: 825
succedat pugnae Troianosque arceat urbe.
iamque vale.' simul his dictis linquebat habenas
ad terram non sponte fluens. tum frigida toto
paulatim exsolvit se corpore, lentaque colla
et captum leto posuit caput, arma relinquens,   830
vitaque cum gemitu fugit indignata sub umbras.
tum vero immensus surgens ferit aurea clamor
sidera: deiecta crudescit pugna Camilla;
incurrunt densi simul omnis copia Teucrum
Tyrrhenique duces Euandrique Arcades alae.   835

836–915: Opis, when she sees Camilla die, promises her fame and vengeance. She kills Arruns. The Latins are routed and flee back to Laurentum, where there is chaos and bloodshed. Turnus abandons his ambush and withdraws to the city. Aeneas and his men climb through the pass. Night falls.

**A
Level**

Commentary Notes

An asterisk (*) is used to indicate stylistic features that are listed in the Introduction.

At the end of Book X, in the course of a fierce battle between the Trojans and their Italian enemies, Aeneas killed first the young Lausus and then his father, Mezentius.

1–99

After setting up a trophy with the arms of the dead Mezentius, Aeneas mourns over the body of Pallas as it is readied for the procession that will convey it to his father, Evander, at Pallanteum for burial.

1 A formulaic clause to mark the start of a new day, modelled on Homer's similar formulae. The natural word order (*Aurora Oceanum reliquit*) is inverted. **Oceanum** – Virgil is following the Greek belief that there was a 'river of Ocean' that encircled the earth. Since the sun was thought to rise at the eastern edge of the world, it would always emerge from the eastern part of the ocean. Since the Trojans are encamped on the west coast of Italy, for them the sun would rise over the coastal plain of Latium. **Aurora** – personified like *Oceanum*: the Roman mythological tradition was that Aurora was a goddess whose job it was to rise in the East to herald the approach of the sun.

2–4 quamquam . . . praecipitant curae – 'although his anxieties urge (him)'. **et** – here 'also' (i.e. as well as setting up a trophy). **sociis . . . humandis** – dative of purpose: 'for burying his comrades'. **turbata funere** – his mind is 'troubled by (thoughts of) death'. **mens est** – '(although) it was his mind', i.e. intention. **Aeneas . . . vota deum . . .**

AS

solvebat – 'Aeneas began to fulfil his vows to the gods'. **deum** = *deorum*; the genitive is either possessive (as vows belong to the gods) or objective (the gods receive the vows). This activity was a standard feature of ancient religious practice: when a man prayed for something, he would promise a gift to the god in return; custom dictated that this vow should take precedence over other activities. Aeneas had promised to set up a trophy before killing Lausus. **victor** – 'because he was the victor' (in apposition to *Aeneas*). **primo . . . Eoo** – Eous was the Morning Star, and so represents dawn: 'at the first sign of Dawn'. Note that the emphasis in this first part of the book is on Aeneas' *pius* or 'dutiful' side, rather than on his prowess and ruthlessness in battle, which was the theme in Book X. These two elements of his character are interwoven throughout the *Aeneid*, making him a much more complex and rounded hero than those of the *Iliad*.

5 Note the slow rhythm of this line. **ingentem** – hyperbole*, as the tree trunk had to be small enough to manoeuvre into place and dress with arms. **quercum** – the object of *constituit*.

6 constituit – here 'he set upright'; clearly the oak tree has been cut down and then shorn of its branches. **tumulo** – 'on a mound' (ablative of place). **induit** – 'he dressed it in'.

7 Mezenti – Mezentius was an Etruscan king, who had been exiled by his own people because of his cruelty, and fled to the territory of the Rutuli, where Turnus made him an ally. **exuvias, tropaeum** – both are in apposition to *arma*. **tibi, magne** – an example of apostrophe*; the trophy is to be offered to Mars, the god of War, described here as *bellipotens*.

8 cristas – these are the plumes that form a crest on Mezentius' helmet.

9 telaque trunca – the spears of a defeated enemy were ritually broken before being added to a trophy.

AS

9-10 The order is *et thoraca petitum perfossumque bis sex locis.* **thoraca** – the ending is a Greek accusative singular, equivalent to *thoracem.*

10-11 ex aere – 'made of bronze'. **sinistrae, collo** – the trunk of the oak tree, now it is dressed, is treated as if a human body; *sinistrae* is dative dependent on *subligat*: 'fastened to the left side'; *collo* is ablative: 'from the neck'. **eburnum** – 'ivory-hilted'.

12-13 socios ... ovantes – his allies are 'triumphant' because they are celebrating the setting up of the trophy and so the death of their powerful enemy. **omnis ... turba ducum** – i.e. all the allied commanders, including the Etruscans, who were particularly delighted by the death of Mezentius. **stipata ... turba** – 'the crowd packed around (him)'. **tegebat** – lit. 'was covering' or 'was protecting'; here 'was surrounding'.

14 effecta – supply *est*. The achievement he speaks of is the killing of Mezentius. **abesto** – this is the third person imperative form of *absum*: 'let (all fear) be absent'.

15 quod superest – the antecedent of *quod* is to be supplied (e.g. *de eo*): 'in respect of what remains (to be done)'.

16 primitiae – 'the first-fruits of war', defining *spolia*; although Aeneas had already killed many enemy soldiers, Mezentius was the first major opponent he had killed, and this was the first trophy he had set up. **manibusque meis** – ablative of instrument: 'achieved by my hands'. **hic** – the trophy takes the form of Mezentius.

17 nunc iter ... nobis – supply *faciendum est*. **regem** – Latinus. **murosque Latinos** – Laurentum.

18 arma parate animis – note the strong assonance*. Note also that the line forms a perfect chiasmus (a, b, c *et* c, b, a)*. **animis** – 'with courage'; **spe** – 'with hope' (instrumental ablatives).

AS

19–21 The order is *ne qua mora impediat (nos) ignaros.* **ignaros** – here 'unready'. **vellere signa** – 'to pull up the standards'; the *signa* consisted of emblems fixed to poles and represented rallying points for the soldiers, who were trained to follow them. When no battle was being fought, the standards were fixed in the ground; when battle commenced, they were pulled up. **adnuerint superi** – '(when first) the gods give their assent'; auspices had to be taken before a battle to establish that it was not ill-omened. **castris** – ablative of separation. **segnis sententia** – 'a feeling of reluctance'. **metu** – ablative of cause. **tardet** – supply *nos*.

22–3 socios inhumataque corpora – 'our allies and (their) unburied bodies', i.e. 'the unburied bodies of our allies' (hendiadys*). The exhortation picks up from lines 2–3. **mandemus** – 'let us commit', i.e. for burial. **solus honos** – the Romans and before them the Greeks believed that without a burial rite, the soul of a dead person was doomed to wander the Earth for a hundred years before gaining admission to the Underworld; cf. Book VI, 325 (*inhumataque turba*) and the plot of Sophocles' play *Antigone*. **Acheronte sub imo** – lit. 'below the deepest Acheron', i.e. 'down in the depths of the Underworld'; the Acheron was one of the five mythical rivers of the Underworld, and here stands for the Underworld as a whole (synecdoche*).

24–6 The order is *decorate egregias animas, quae ..., supremis muneribus.* **decorate** – here 'honour'. **supremis muneribus** – the 'last rites' are the burials. **sanguine ... suo** – ablative of instrument. **hanc patriam peperere** – *peperere* = *pepererunt*: '(who) have created this (to be) our homeland'.

26–7 The order is (and) *primus Pallas mittatur ad maestam urbem Euandri.* **mittatur** – 'let him be sent'. Note the heavy alliteration* of *m* in these lines. **quem** – this is the object of both *abstulit* and *mersit.* **non virtutis egentem** – 'not lacking in courage' (litotes*).

AS

28 atra dies – *dies* may be masculine or feminine; in Roman calendars unlucky days were marked in black. **funere acerbo** – instrumental ablative. This line is a repeat of Book VI, 429, giving it a slightly formulaic quality.

29 recipitque . . . gressum – 'and retraced his step'. **ad limina** – 'to the entrance' (of his house or tent, depending on whether the Trojans had got as far as building individual houses inside their camp).

30–1 corpus ubi = *ubi corpus*. **positum** – 'laid out', ready for burial. **Acoetes . . . senior** – *senior* does not usually bear its comparative meaning, simply meaning 'old' or 'elderly'. **servabat** – 'watched over'.

31–2 Parrhasio Euandro – Parrhasia was a town in Arcadia (in Greece), which had been Evander's homeland before moving to Italy. These two words 'break' the rules for the dactylic hexameter (see Introduction): the *-o* at the end of *Parrhăsĭo* gives a hiatus: it cannot elide (as that would leave too few syllables to complete the line); also *-o Euandro* gives a spondee in the fifth foot. This combination occurs only five times in the whole *Aeneid* (usually with Greek names), but is more common in Homer. **armiger** – this was a servant whose job it was to look after the armour and weapons of a leading warrior, like the medieval squire.

32–3 The order is *sed tum, datus comes caro alumno, ibat non aeque felicibus auspiciis*, i.e. the omens were not as favourable as when he had served Evander. **comes** – 'as companion'.

34–5 circum – supply *stabant*. **famulum** – archaic genitive plural. **-que . . . -que** – 'both . . . and', with the first one delayed to make *omnis* qualify both *manus* and *turba*. **maestum crinem solutae** – lit. 'loosened with respect to their sad hair', and so 'with their hair let down in mourning'. *Crinem* is variously explained as a retained accusative after a passive verb; or an accusative of respect; or an

48   *Virgil* Aeneid *XI*

adverbial accusative. It is however perhaps best viewed as a borrowing from the Greek middle verb construction, in which *solutae* is treated as if active in meaning, like a deponent verb; *crinem* then becomes the direct object. This is one of Virgil's favourite constructions; readers will be referred back to this note for future instances. **maestum** – hypallage*. **de more** – 'according to custom'.

36 ut – 'when' (taking the indicative). **foribus ... altis** – probably dative with the compound verb; alternatively ablative of route taken. This phrase may indicate that Aeneas' home was a house rather than a tent (cf. line 29).

37–8 tunsis ... pectoribus – the ablative absolute may be translated as if present active; the beating of breasts was a ritual expression of mourning for both men and women. **maestoque immugit regia luctu** – *immugit* is a strong, onomatopoeic* verb, suggesting the bellowing of cattle; it is translatable here as 'resounded'; note also the consonance*, and the enclosing word-order*. **regia** – simply the 'abode of the king', whether tent or something grander.

39 nivei ... Pallantis – his skin has the pallor of death, following the loss of blood; the adjective may also suggest innocence and purity.

40 ut – 'when', as in line 36. **patens ... vulnus** – 'the wound gaping open'. **levi ... in pectore** – this is lēvi, not lĕvi (as the metre dictates), and so 'smooth', suggesting that Pallas was too young to have developed body hair.

41 cuspidis Ausoniae – '(the wound) caused by the Italian javelin'; the genitive is subjective, as the javelin caused the wound; Ausonia was a poetic name for South Italy. Note the fast rhythm of this line.

42–3 tene – the position of *te* is emphatic at the start of the line and speech: 'was it you ...?' **cum laeta veniret** – supply *Fortuna* as the subject of *veniret*, just as it is the subject of *invidit*; *laeta* has the idea of 'bringing joy'. Fortune (thought of as a deity) brought him good luck in that he won the battle, but bad luck in that he lost Pallas. **ne** – the negative purpose clause depends on *invidit*: Fortune begrudged Aeneas the life of Pallas, so that Pallas might not see the Trojan mission (*regna . . . nostra*) completed.

44 veherere = *vehereris* (second singular imperfect subjunctive passive): a second negative purpose clause. **victor** – 'as victor', and so 'in victory'. **ad sedes . . . paternas** – i.e. Pallanteum.

45–6 non haec . . . promissa . . . dederam – 'this is not what I had promised'. *non haec* is an example of litotes*. Aeneas had in fact promised Evander that he would look after Pallas. **me . . . euntem** – 'me as I left'.

47 Note the very heavy alliteration* of *m-*, added to that of *v-*, *p-* and then *d-* in the preceding lines, all underlining the powerful emotions of grief and bitterness. **in imperium** – 'to win an empire'.

48 viros – i.e. the enemy. **proelia** – supply *esse* again. **dura . . . gente** – the metre makes *dura* agree with *gente*, not *proelia*.

49 ille quidem – 'he certainly' (meaning Evander), contrasted with *nos* in line 51. **multum** – 'completely' (adverb). **captus** – 'taken in' or 'deceived'.

50 Note the chiasmus* in *vota facit cumulatque altaria*.

51–2 nos . . . maesti comitamur – '(while) we sadly accompany'. **iuvenem exanimum et** – it is unusual to have two consecutive accusative endings eliding before vowels. **nil iam caelestibus ullis debentem** – 'now owing no debt to any of the heavenly gods'; in contrast with Evander, who is probably still making vows to the gods for his son's safe return (*vota facit*), Pallas, being dead, has no such obligations. **vano . . . honore** – this phrase, enclosing *maesti*

AS

comitamur, must indicate how Aeneas and his people will accompany the body: 'with empty honour', i.e. the honour they have achieved in winning the overall battle is rendered nought by the death of Pallas.

53 infelix – Aeneas is addressing Evander as if he were present (apostrophe*). Note the heavily spondaic rhythm of this line.

54–5 These are rhetorical questions*. Supply *sunt* with the first two clauses and *est* with the third. **nostri reditus** – 'our return' (plural for singular), i.e. the return of both Aeneas and Pallas to Pallanteum. **exspectatique triumphi** – the two men had hoped to return to Pallanteum in triumph after defeating the Latins and Rutulians. **magna fides** – the 'strong pledge' is the one made by Aeneas to Evander in Book VIII to look after Pallas.

55–6 at – introduces Aeneas' one consolation, that Pallas has not died a coward's death from *pudendis vulneribus* ('shameful wounds'), i.e. wounds in the back as he ran away. **aspicies** – supply *eum*. Note the heavy alliteration* and consonance* with *p*, marking Aeneas' bitterness.

56–7 'nor will you wish for a dreadful death as a father when his son is safe'; a heroic death was considered far preferable to a cowardly death, which, according to heroic convention, would have heaped so much shame upon the dead man's father that he too would have wanted to die.

57–8 quantum praesidium – Aeneas suggests that, had Pallas lived, he would have become a champion protector of Southern Italy. **Ausonia** – supply *perdis*; in full this would be *quantum praesidium tu, Ausonia, perdis, et quantum praesidium tu, Iule, perdis* (suggesting that Iulus would have had a powerful supporter, had Pallas lived); it is possible, however, that the second *quantum* should be taken on its own: 'and how big your loss is, Iulus'. Iulus was Aeneas' son, whom Aeneas hoped would succeed him as ruler of the Trojans.

AS

59 haec ubi deflevit – *ubi* should be taken first: lit. 'when he wept over these things', and so 'when he had spoken these words in lamentation'. **tolli** – the passive infinitive may be used with *impero* instead of the more common *ut* and subjunctive.

60–2 The order is *et ex toto agmine mittit mille lectos viros, qui . . .* **qui . . . comitentur . . . intersint** – the relative and subjunctives express purpose. **supremum . . . honorem** – 'the last honour' for the dead man is his funeral procession.

62–3 solacia luctus exigua ingentis – the interlocked word order is an example of synchysis*; note also the effect of juxtaposing the two adjectives (antithesis*). *Solacia* is either in loose apposition to *qui* (the thousand men will be a solace) or even more loosely to the action of accompanying the funeral procession. **debita** – no matter how inadequate the *solacia*, it was owed to Evander because of Aeneas' promise.

64 haud segnes – 'not slow', i.e. very quickly (litotes*). **crates et molle feretrum** – lit. 'wickerwork and a soft bier', and so 'a soft bier of wickerwork' (Williams). This is an example of hendiadys*; perhaps also hypallage* if translated as 'a bier of soft wickerwork'.

65 arbuteis . . . virgis – the arbutus or strawberry tree is native to southern Europe. **vimine querno** – singular for plural: 'with oak twigs'; *vimen* is a pliant twig used for basketwork.

66 exstructosque toros – plural for singular; the 'couch' is the top surface of the bier, 'built up high' ready to receive the body. **obtentu** – 'with a canopy' (ablative of instrument).

67 iuvenem . . . sublimem – although this could mean 'the distinguished youth', the position of *sublimem*, framed by *agresti stramine*, indicates that the word has its basic meaning of 'high up'. **agresti . . . stramine** – 'on the rustic bed'; it is rustic because it is assembled from undressed timber. *Stramen* is literally 'straw', and the phrase could mean 'on the rustic bed of straw', indicating that the surface of the bier was covered with straw so that the body would lie on softer material than bare wood. Most editors, however, interpret *stramen* to mean the whole bier.

68–71 qualem – introduces an epic simile*, poignantly comparing the body of Pallas to a flower plucked (*demessum*, from *demeto*) by a maiden that has not yet lost its freshness; *qualem* is accusative to agree with *florem*, which in turn is the object of *alit* and *ministrat*.

68 virgineo . . . pollice – 'by the thumb of a maiden', loosely used to mean 'by the fingers' or 'between the finger and thumb' of a maiden.

69–70 seu . . . seu – giving two possible definitions of *florem*. **violae . . . hyacinthi** – although these names probably do not coincide with their usage today, it is acceptable to translate them as 'violet' and 'hyacinth'. **languentis** – 'drooping', suggesting a natural habit of growth rather than that it was wilting. Scanning this line will show that the final syllable of *languentis* breaks the rule for determining syllable length: the genitive singular ending *-is* is naturally short, and should be so here, as the *h-* of *hyacinthi* is ignored. This is not carelessness on the part of Virgil; rather he is copying a Greek exception to the rule, known as 'lengthening in arsis', probably because *hyacinthus* is a Greek word and because the last syllable of *languentis* carries heavy stress. **neque . . . adhuc nec dum** – 'neither yet . . . nor yet'.

71 mater . . . tellus – 'mother earth': earth was seen as the 'mother' of all plant life.

72 geminas vestes – 'a pair of garments' or perhaps 'matching garments'. **auroque ostroque** – polysyndeton*; causal ablatives; purple was an expensive dye reserved for the use of royalty, and so equated in importance to gold.

AS

73-5 The order is *quas Sidonia Dido ipsa, laeta laborum, quondam fecerat illi suis manibus*. **Sidonia Dido** – Dido was queen of Carthage (on the North African coast), where the Trojans were shipwrecked while on their way to Italy. Dido entertained Aeneas and fell in love with him. As an expression of her love she had made these richly-embroidered garments for Aeneas. She is called 'Sidonian' because, before sailing away to found Carthage, she had been a member of the royal family in Phoenicia (modern Lebanon), of which Sidon was one of the principal cities. **laeta laborum** – 'rejoicing in her work'; the genitive is unusual: it is either a poetic usage expressing cause, or it is modelled on the objective genitive (where the work would be the object of her enjoyment). **et tenui telas discreverat auro** – 'and (she) had interwoven the warp with threads of gold'; the warp is the row of longitudinal threads (here of purple) fixed to the loom; the 'fine gold', i.e. gold threads, therefore formed part of the weft, the transverse thread that is attached to the moving shuttle.

76 The subject is Aeneas, described as *maestus* (best translated here as an adverb). **harum** – supply *vestium*. **supremum honorem** – the same idea as in line 61; here it is in apposition to *unam*.

77 arsuras comas – 'the hair that would burn (on the pyre)'. **amictu** – this is the second garment, the first having been placed over or round the body.

78 multa ... praemia – 'many spoils' from the battle that had just been fought on the plain between the Trojan camp and the Latin city of Laurentum. It was customary for the victorious leaders to share out the spoils amongst themselves; they would consist of armour stripped from the bodies of the slain enemy. **Laurentis ... pugnae** – 'from the battle fought against the people of Laurentum'.

79 praedam – this is the same as the *praemia*: as well as piling it up, Aeneas ordered it to be brought out in a long line.

AS

80 equos et tela – these would be burnt on the pyre along with the corpse, to provide the spirit of the dead man with what he would need in the after-life. **quibus spoliaverat hostem** – 'of which he had despoiled the enemy', and so 'which he had stripped from the enemy'; *hostem* is a collective singular; *quibus* is an ablative of separation.

81–2 vinxerat et – *et* should be taken first; the subject of *vinxerat* and *mitteret* is Aeneas, who had taken personal responsibility for the funeral rites. **manus, quos** – in full this would be *manus eorum, quos*. **quos mitteret** – 'whom he would send': subjunctive of purpose. **umbris inferias** – 'as offerings to the spirits of the Underworld'; *inferias* (in apposition to *quos*) are sacrifices to the dead. **sparsurus** – 'intending to sprinkle'. **caeso . . . sanguine** – lit. 'with slain blood' and so 'with the blood of the slain men' (this is akin to hypallage*, in which the adjective (*caeso*) is transferred from the men to their blood). Aeneas had already prepared for this human sacrifice in Book X when he took the men prisoner. This episode is modelled on Homer, *Iliad* XXI and XXIII, where Achilles sacrificed Trojan prisoners at the funeral of his young friend Patroclus, who had been killed by the Trojan leader, Hector. In the *Aeneid*, Pallas is the counterpart of Patroclus. The sacrifice in the *Iliad* was horrifying enough; here it seems worse, as it is so alien to Roman morality.

83–4 truncos – like the trophy already described in 5–11; *truncos* is the object of *ferre*. **ipsos ferre duces** – the emphatic position of *ipsos* indicates that this was an unusual honour for Pallas. The arms adorning these tree trunks would have belonged to men killed by Pallas. **inimicaque nomina figi** – 'and (he ordered) that the names of the enemies be affixed (to the trophies)'; Virgil takes it for granted that writing was known at this time.

85 ducitur . . . Acoetes – Pallas' old armour-bearer has to be helped along because of his age and grief.

AS

86 foedans – Acoetes is 'defiling' his breast by beating it, a standard ritual of mourning. **unguibus ora** – note the chiastic* word order, being in reverse order to *pectora pugnis*.

87 sternitur et – parallel to *ducitur*: one moment he is helped to walk, the next he collapses; *et* should be taken first. **toto proiectus corpore** – lit. 'having been thrown forward with his whole body', and so 'flinging himself full length'. **terrae** – dative, equivalent to *ad terram*.

88 ducunt – the subject is the Trojans in general. **currus** – these must be chariots that Pallas had captured after killing their occupants. Virgil, like Homer before him, presents chariot-fighting as a standard part of any battle; chariots carried two occupants: the driver and the warrior. **Rutulo perfusos sanguine** – 'soaked in Rutulian blood'; note the enclosing word-order*.

89–90 bellator equus – Pallas' 'war horse'. **positis insignibus** – 'its trappings laid aside', as being no longer needed. **Aethon** – the name is Greek, meaning 'Fiery'; in *Iliad* VIII one of Hector's horses was called Aethon. **lacrimans** – the image is taken from *Iliad* XVII.

91 cetera – i.e. Pallas' sword and sword-belt, the seizure of which contributed to Turnus' death at the hands of Aeneas at the end of the *Aeneid*.

92–3 phalanx – the phalanx was a dense formation of soldiers lined up in battle formation. To accompany a funeral procession with a formal arrangement like this was a sign of respect for the dead man. **Teucrique ... Tyrrenique omnes et ... Arcades** – these are all in apposition to *phalanx*, defining its content; this is an example of polysyndeton*; *Teucri* is one of several names Virgil uses for the Trojans, taken from Teucer, one of the early kings of Troy. **versis ... armis** – 'with their arms reversed', i.e. with their spears pointing backwards, as a sign of mourning.

AS

94 omnis ... ordo – 'the whole line (of mourners)'. **praecesserat** – 'had led the way': the funeral procession (described in lines 79–92) that would accompany the body to Pallanteum went first and was followed by the 'phalanx'.

95 haec – supply *verba*.

96 The order is *eadem horrida fata belli vocant nos hinc ad alias lacrimas*. The 'same dreadful fates of war' refers to the large number of other dead Trojans and their allies that await burial (cf. lines 2–3). **ad alias lacrimas** – 'to other tears' of lamentation as they bury their other comrades.

97–8 salve ... vale – the invocation 'hail and farewell' was regularly used at funerals, as a final greeting; the words more commonly used are *(h)ave atque vale* (as in Catullus CI and many inscriptions). **aeternum** – used adverbially to mean 'for ever' (also in Catullus CI). **mihi** – this is the so-called 'ethic' dative, modelled on a Greek usage, used to state a person who has an interest in the action but does not have a syntactical relationship with the rest of the clause; translate as 'I pray'.

99 muros – these are the walls of the *castra*.

100–38

A truce is agreed between the Latins and the Trojans to allow the collection and burial of the dead.

100 oratores – lit. 'speakers', and so 'ambassadors'. **ex urbe Latina** – i.e. Laurentum.

101 velati ramis oleae – olive branches were a traditional symbol of peace; here, being carried in the ambassadors' hands, they 'overshadowed' them. **veniam** – either 'an indulgence' or 'permission' to collect the bodies.

102–3 corpora redderet – in full this would be something like *Aenean rogaverunt ut corpora sibi redderet*; this is a shortened indirect command, as found in continuing oratio obliqua. **per . . . iacebant** – the order is *quae, fusa ferro, iacebant per campos*. **ferro . . . fusa** – 'laid low by the sword'. **sineret** – this continues the indirect command. **tumulo . . . succedere terrae** – here 'to be placed (lit. 'to go') under a mound of earth'; *tumulo* is dative dependent on the compound verb.

104 nullum certamen – indirect statement, which in full would be *negaverunt ullum certamen esse*. **et aethere cassis** – 'and with those deprived of the upper world': *aether*, as well as its basic meaning of 'air' is also used by Virgil (e.g. Book VI, 436) to mean the world above, as opposed to the Underworld. The argument of the ambassadors is that the Trojans can have no enmity left with those defeated and killed; these are not to be seen as two distinct groups, but as a single group of men defeated and then killed.

105 parceret – another indirect command. **hospitibus quondam** – 'people who once gave them hospitality': when the Trojans first landed in Latium (Book VII), King Latinus initially welcomed them and offered Aeneas the hand of his daughter Lavinia in marriage; this was before the goddess Juno turned local opinion against the Trojans. **socerisque vocatis** – 'and men (once) called "father-in-law"': while the Latins were still well-disposed towards the Trojans, many of them were prepared to offer their daughters in marriage to the Trojans; the perfect tense implies that some of these relationships had already begun before the Latins turned on their guests.

106 haud aspernanda precantes – '(since they were) requesting things that could not be refused'; *precantes* agrees with *quos*.

AS

107 prosequitur venia – 'he presented them with permission', and so 'he granted them permission'. **verbis ... addit** – 'and to his words he added ...'. The *verbis* are the words with which he granted permission to collect the bodies. Note the chiasmus* (*prosequitur venia ... verbis addit*).

108-9 The order is *quaenam indigna fortuna, Latini, implicuit vos tanto bello*. **indigna** – here 'cruel'. **qui nos fugiatis amicos** – 'that you shun us as friends' (a result clause introduced by *tanto ... qui* instead of *tanto ... ut*).

110-11 exanimis et ... peremptis – 'for the dead and those killed'; the words relate to *victis* and *cassis* in 104 (see note above). **oratis** – the enjambment* adds heavy emphasis to this word, which as a result is given an artificially lengthened final syllable (cf. 69); the tone is ironic. **equidem** – although this word is supposedly derived from *e* + *quidem*, Virgil always uses it as if it were derived from *ego* + *quidem*, meaning 'I for my part', used to contrast what the speaker does or says with what others have said or done (here *oratis*). **et vivis concedere vellem** – 'would have wished to grant (peace) also to the living'; *et* = *etiam*; *vellem* is a potential subjunctive.

112 nec veni, nisi fata ... dedissent – 'I would not have come, had not fate granted ...'; this combination of indicative and subjunctive in a conditional sentence is very unusual (*venissem* would have been normal); it is as if Aeneas changed his mind half-way through, beginning with the idea that he only came to fulfil his destiny, and then changed his mind to say that he would not have come, if fate had not granted him a home. **locum sedemque** – 'a place for a home' (hendiadys*). **fata** – throughout the *Aeneid* Virgil presents Aeneas as being driven and directed by 'the fates' (nearly always treated as plural in the *Aeneid*), which may be viewed as an abstract concept of the fate that determines all human actions, or the personified

AS

Fates, three sisters in Greek mythology who spun out the lives of all humans.

113–14 cum gente – Aeneas has no quarrel with the Latin people as a whole: it was their king who renounced their friendship. **nostra . . . hospitia** – 'our ties of friendship'.

115 aequius fuerat – 'it would have been fairer'; the indicative is preferred in this and similar expressions, despite its being equivalent to a past unfulfilled condition. **se opponere** – 'to expose himself'. **huic . . . morti** – 'to this death'; Aeneas points to the corpses as he speaks.

116 manu – either 'by force of arms' or 'in hand-to-hand combat' – both equally possible.

117 decuit – 'it was his duty', i.e. when the war broke out. **his . . . telis** – 'with these weapons'; again Aeneas points to the objects.

118 vixet – a contraction of *vixisset*; supply *is*: 'the one would have lived to whom . . .'; the pluperfect subjunctive forms the apodosis of a past unfulfilled condition, the protasis of which is to be inferred: 'if he had fought me in this way'. **deus aut sua dextra** – the outcome of a heroic battle was never determined by human action alone: the gods or fate always took a hand.

119 et miseris supponite civibus ignem – 'and light the pyre beneath your poor citizens'; *civibus* is dative with the compound verb.

120 obstipuēre – an alternative form of *obstipuerunt*, frequent in poetry (there are many further examples of this contraction in the text; they will not be pointed out again). The ambassadors are astonished because Aeneas has presented himself as fair-minded, and not at all as the ruthless enemy they had expected.

121 conversique – 'and turning round'. **inter se** – 'towards each other'. Perhaps better might be 'and they kept their eyes and faces turned

AS

towards each other', where *conversi* could be construed as being modelled on the Greek middle verb (cf. 35 note). The idea is that the ambassadors were ashamed to meet Aeneas' gaze, because his words had clearly set him morally above them.

122–4 senior . . . Drances – 'the elderly Drances', with *senior* contrasted with *iuveni* in the same position in the next line. Drances has not appeared previously in the *Aeneid*, but plays an important role in 336ff. **odiis et crimine . . . infensus** – 'showing his hostility [towards Turnus] with hatred and accusations'. Virgil compares the old Drances unfavourably with the young Turnus, despite the latter being the number one enemy of the Trojans; in heroic terms, Turnus is more open and honourable than Drances. **sic ore vicissim orsa refert** – lit. 'thus gave back beginnings in turn with his mouth'; this singularly Virgilian expression may be translated 'began to speak thus in response'.

124–5 o fama ingens, ingentior armis – *fama* is ablative, giving a chiastic* order to these words: 'O (man) great in glory, greater in battle'. The ablatives are of respect. **quibus caelo te laudibus aequem** – lit. 'with what praises am I to make you equal to the sky?'; this extravagant rhetorical question* can be understood to mean 'what praises can I use to exalt you to the sky?' **aequem** – deliberative subjunctive, as is *mirer* below.

126 – 'Am I to marvel at you first for your justice or for your exertions in war?' **-ne . . . -ne** – an alternative to *utrum . . . an* introducing alternative questions. **iustitiae . . . laborum** – the genitives are very unusual, being modelled on Greek causal genitives. **mirer** – supply *te* as the object. **belli** – genitive of definition.

127–9 nos vero – 'we for our part', marking a transition from the lavish praise of Aeneas to how the ambassadors intend to respond. **haec** – supply *verba*. **patriam . . . ad urbem** – i.e. to Laurentum.

AS

et te ... Latino iungemus regi – 'and we shall unite you with king Latinus', i.e. they will try to revive the original alliance agreed between the Latins and Trojans. **si qua viam dederit fortuna** – 'if any fortune provides a way'; *fortuna* here is good luck, which will be needed if the ambassadors are to succeed. **quaerat sibi foedera Turnus** – 'let Turnus seek treaties for himself', i.e. without our help.

130–1 quin et – short for *quin etiam*: 'indeed ... even', introducing the climax to Drances' ornate and extravagant speech. **fatales murorum ... moles** – lit. 'the fated masses of walls', and so 'the massive walls decreed by fate'; the walls are 'decreed by fate' because the Trojans had told Latinus as much when they first approached him for help. **attollere ... subvectare** – both infinitives are dependent on the impersonal *iuvabit*. **saxa ... Troiana** – 'Trojan stones', because the stones will be used to build a new city for the Trojans.

132 dixerat – Virgil regularly uses the pluperfect tense at the conclusion of a speech. Translate as 'he finished speaking'. **omnes ... fremebant** – 'all (the ambassadors) loudly spoke'; *fremebant* is a strong word in an emphatic position. **uno ... ore** – 'with one voice'.

133 bis senos pepigere dies – 'they made an agreement for twelve days'. **pace sequestra** – 'with the peace as guarantor', i.e. 'under the protection of the truce'.

135–6 iugis – the woods were on the mountain ridges, presumably the Alban Hills, though apparently there were densely wooded marshes much closer to hand. They needed timber for the funeral pyres. **alta ... fraxinus** – the *fraxinus* was a remarkably slender, and so relatively tall, ash tree. **ferro ... bipenni** – *bipennis* is most often used as a feminine noun; here it must have its basic adjectival force to agree with *ferro*: 'double-bladed'. **actas ad sidera** – 'soaring upwards to the stars'.

AS

137–8 The order is *nec cessant scindere cuneis robora et olentem cedrum, nec (cessant) vectare ornos gementibus plaustris.* **cuneis** – wedges were hammered into logs to split them into planks. **robora** – here 'oak trees' rather than general timber as frequently. **plaustris . . . gementibus** – the wagons are 'groaning' under the weight of the cut timber.

139–81

Evander learns of the death of his son and mourns deeply for him.

139–40 Fama – Rumour is frequently personified in the *Aeneid*; in Book IV (173ff) Virgil devotes sixteen lines to describing the deity, as a monstrous, ever-wakeful and multi-tongued creature that preys on mankind. **Euandrum . . . replet** – Rumour 'fills Evander', meaning either that she fills his ears with the news, or that she fills him with grief.

141 quae – the antecedent is *Fama*. **Latio** – local ablative. **ferebat** – 'brought the news of'. Rumour could spread both good news and bad.

142–3 ruĕre . . . rapuēre – *ruĕre* is a historic infinitive. **funereas faces** – torches traditionally played an important role in Roman funerals, with four being placed at the corners of the bier, and then many being carried during the funeral procession through the streets.

143–4 via . . . discriminat – lit. 'the road distinguishes the fields', i.e. the light cast by the torches moving along the road 'distinguishes' and so 'picks out' or 'lights up' the fields on either side; translate as 'the road was illuminated . . . and this picked out . . .'

145–6 contra . . . veniens – the thousand men sent by Aeneas to accompany the body of Pallas came 'to meet them', though in reality it was Evander and his people who came to meet the Trojan procession. **plangentia ... agmina** – 'the throng of mourners'.

146–7 quae – a connecting relative, the antecedent of which is *agmina*. **matres** – since the soldiers who had died were all young men, they were mourned by mothers rather than wives; it was not customary for fathers to show their grief in public. **maestam incendunt clamoribus urbem** – 'they set the sad city aflame with their cries'; the verb provides a powerful metaphor*; *maestam* is an example of hypallage*, more logically defining the cries.

148–9 potis est – archaic for *potest*. **in medios** – supply *homines* or similar.

149–50 The order is *feretro reposto, (Euander) procubuit super Pallanta*. **feretro ... reposto** – 'when the bier had been set down'; *reposto* = *reposito*. **haeret** – 'clung to him' (a favourite word of Virgil).

151 via vix ... voci laxata ... est – 'a way was with difficulty opened up for his voice', i.e. he could barely speak because of his grief. Note the heavy alliteration*.

152 non haec ... dederas promissa – 'this was not the promise you had given'; *non haec* is emphatic. **petenti** – the manuscripts all read *parenti* ('to your father'), but *petenti* (mentioned by Servius) gives better sense: 'to (me) pleading', and so 'to my plea that you should ...'

153 ut – to be taken first; the word order emphasizes *cautius* ('more cautiously' than he otherwise would). **saevo ... Marti** – 'to savage warfare'.

154–5 haud ignarus eram – litotes*: 'I knew full well'. **quantum ... posset** – 'how much influence (new glory etc.) could have'. **praedulce decus** – 'very sweet honour', a second subject of *posset*, parallel to *nova* *gloria.* Evander's argument is that a young warrior's first victory in battle can too easily go to his head and lead him to recklessness.

156–7 primitiae . . . miserae, dura rudimenta – these are vocatives, addressed in exclamation; *primitiae* are the 'first-fruits' and so the 'first victory' of war; *rudimenta* are 'first attempts' at warfare; they are 'hard' because they have led to an early death. **belli propinqui** – the fact that Pallas' first and fatal experience of war was so close to home makes it seem worse.

157–8 nulli exaudita deorum – '(vows and prayers) heeded by none of the gods'; *nulli* is dative of the agent dependent on a perfect passive participle. **vota precesque meae** – vocatives.

159 felix morte tua – 'fortunate in your death'; this is the only occasion that Virgil mentions Evander's dead wife. **neque in hunc servata dolorem** – 'nor kept alive to see this grief', giving the reason for her good fortune.

160–1 vivendo vici mea fata – lit. 'I have conquered my destiny by living (on)', and so 'I have outlived my destined life-span'. **restarem ut** – *ut* should be taken first: 'so that I was left surviving'. The argument is that fathers ought not to outlive their sons.

161–2 The order is *Rutuli obruerent telis (me) secutum socia arma Troum.* **secutum** – surprisingly Virgil has omitted the important *me* for *secutum* to agree with, even though his argument is clear enough from what follows: he wishes he had been killed instead of his son. **obruerent** – the unusual use of the imperfect subjunctive has been explained in various ways, most suggesting that it is a more vivid and continuing alternative to the more usual pluperfect, in which case it is probably a past unfulfilled wish ('would that they had overwhelmed me'); alternatively it might be a present unfulfilled wish ('would that they were overwhelming me').

AS

162–3 dedissem . . . referret – each is the apodosis of an unfulfilled condition, the protasis to be inferred from the preceding wish: 'if the Rutuli had overwhelmed me, then I would have given . . . (and this procession) would be bringing me back'; the tenses are perfectly logical. An alternative interpretation is to take the two verbs as parallel to *obruerent*, expressing further unfulfilled wishes.

164–5 arguerim – 'nor would I wish to blame you' (for my son's death); the verb is a 'polite perf. subj. of modest statement' (Page), showing Evander's gentle nature. **foedera . . . dextras** – these are further objects of *arguerim*. **hospitio** – 'in guest-friendship'; this was a key element of human relationships in the heroic age: a man travelling outside his own kingdom could only ensure safe passage by forging alliances with those he met, receiving and offering gifts to seal the relationship; such guest-friendships were generally long-lasting and mutually beneficial (that between Aeneas and Latinus was the exception).

165–6 sors ista – 'that fate', pointing to his son's body. **debita erat** – 'was due', i.e. was only to be expected. **nostrae** – plural for singular.

166–8 manebat – 'awaited', indicative because this actually happened. The order for the rest is *iuvabit (me eum) cecidisse, milibus Volscorum ante caesis, ducentem Teucros in Latium.* **iuvabit** – 'it will please me that he . . .' **ante** – i.e. before his death. **ducentem . . . Teucros** – strictly speaking Pallas was not a leader of Trojans, because he had brought his own troops with him; but as a leader allied to the Trojans, he is thought of as sharing the leadership of the whole army.

169–71 digner – 'I would think you worthy of', followed by the ablative. **non alio . . . quam** – 'no other (death) than'. **quam pius Aeneas** – 'than the one dutiful Aeneas (would have thought you worthy of)'; *pius* is Virgil's regular epithet to describe Aeneas, to reflect his dutifulness towards the gods, his people and his allies. Evander does not stop at Aeneas but builds to a rhetorical climax with a

AS

tetracolon (cf. tricolon*). **Tyrrheni . . . Tyrrhenum** – these Etruscans had made an alliance with the Trojans in Book VIII.

172 quos – there are two explanations of this difficult word: either it stands for *ei quos*, and means 'they whom (you killed) bring great trophies', in the sense that the dead Latins are seen as bringing themselves in the form of trophies (tree trunks dressed in their armour); or it stands for *eorum quos*, meaning 'they (the Trojans and their allies) bring trophies of those whom (you killed)'. The Latin lends itself more readily to the former, but the latter gives simpler sense. **dat leto** – lit. 'gives to death' and so 'kills'; *dat* is a vivid present for an action that is purely in the past.

173–5 tu – addresses Turnus (apostrophe*). **stares** – imperfect subjunctive for a present unfulfilled condition. Evander is indulging in wishful thinking, imagining Turnus dead and his armour adorning a tree trunk. **truncus** – in apposition to *tu*. The order for *esset . . . annis* is *si aetas esset par et si robur esset idem ab annis*. **si aetas esset par** – 'if his (Pallas') age were the same (as Turnus')'. **et idem si robur ab annis** – 'and if the strength from his years had been the same (as yours)'; *ab annis* is difficult to construe, but probably dependent on *robur*, signifying the strength that comes from years of maturing. **Turne** – note the heavy emphasis caused by the enjambment*.

175 armis – 'from battle' (ablative of separation).

176 vadite – in his grief Evander has addressed first Pallas, then his wife, then the Trojans, then Pallas again, then Turnus, and now again the Trojans. **haec . . . mandata** – it is this commission that he sends to Aeneas that persuades Aeneas to kill Turnus at the end of Book XII.

177–9 vitam moror invisam – 'I prolong my life, hateful' (because of Pallas' death). **dextera causa tua est** – 'your right hand is the just cause'; *causa* is difficult to explain, but is probably intended to mean that the

Commentary Notes   67

killing of Turnus in retribution is a just cause. **Turnum natoque patrique quam debere vides** – '(your hand) which you see owes (the death of) Turnus to both father and son', i.e. to both Evander and Pallas.

179–80 hic . . . solus . . . locus – 'this is the only course of action' (lit. 'place'). **meritis . . . fortunaeque** – 'to achieve just deserts and good fortune'; the argument is that Aeneas has no alternative but to kill Turnus if he wishes to act honourably and pay off his debt to Evander.

180–1 vitae – 'in (my) life'; now that his son is dead, there can be no more joys in his life. **nec fas** – supply *esset*: 'nor would it be right' (to seek such joys). **perferre** – depends on *quaero*: 'but (what I do seek) is to deliver (the joys to my son)'; *gaudia* are the joys emanating from the news of Turnus' death.

182–224

The scene changes back to the field of battle, where both sides bury their dead.

182–3 almam . . . lucem – 'restorative light' of day; there is a hint of irony in the word *almam*, because the reality was that the return of daylight revealed the huge number of dead bodies awaiting cremation, and so caused the lamentation to break out afresh. Note the heavy alliteration* and consonance* of *m-*. **opera atque labores** – the tasks of collecting and cremating the dead.

184–5 pater Aeneas – Virgil often calls Aeneas *pater* to remind us of the close, caring relationship he had with his people. **Tarchon** – the king and leader of the Etruscans, who made an alliance with Aeneas in Book VIII.

185–6 The order is *quisque tulere* (= *tulerunt*) *huc corpora suorum more patrum.* (Note that *suorum* is best taken with *corpora*, not

AS

patrum.) **tulere:** plural following the sense. **more ... patrum** – the 'custom of their ancestors' was the collection by each man of the bodies of relatives or friends.

186-7 subiectis ignibus – torches were applied to the bases of the pyres. **atris** – as well as its literal meaning of 'murky' (from the smoke), this word should also be taken metaphorically as 'funereal'. **conditur** – the sky is 'buried' in (lit. 'into') darkness. **altum caligine** – the word order and Virgilian usage suggest that *caligine* is dependent upon *altum* rather than being an instrumental ablative qualifying *conditur*: the sky is 'filled to a great height with smoke (lit. 'gloom')'.

188-90 The anaphora* of *ter*, one of Virgil's favourite expressions, emphasizes the ritual nature of the military honours; Homer had a similar ritual for the funeral of Patroclus. **circum accensos ... rogos** – 'round the pyres they had lit'. Note the heavy spondaic rhythm of 188. **decurrere** – a military word to describe troops marching round a pyre in ritual procession; *lustravere* has a similar meaning, but is less technical. **ululatus** – an onomatopoeic* word reflecting the sound of the cries of lamentation. **ore** – ablative of origin.

191 spargitur ... sparguntur – anaphora* with polyptoton*.

192 caelo – poetic for *in caelum*. Note the heavy alliteration* of *c*- and the assonance* of *clamor* and *clangor*, reflecting the sounds. **virum** = *virorum*.

193 hic – 'at this point'. **alii** – 'some', followed in 195 by *pars* ('others').

194-6 igni – 'onto the fire'. The burning of enemy arms on funeral pyres was a Roman custom. **galeas ensesque ... frenaque ... rotas** – all are in apposition to, and explanatory of, *spolia*. **ferventesque rotas** – the chariot wheels are described as 'red-hot' because in use they turn so fast; here the epithet is less appropriate. **pars** – supply *conicit igni* from line 195. **munera nota** – either 'well-known offerings'

or 'traditional offerings' (editorial opinion is divided). **clipeos ...
tela** – in apposition to *munera* (cf. *spolia* above). **ipsorum** – these
shields and spears had belonged to the men whose bodies were being
cremated, rather than being captured armour; this may explain *nota*,
indicating that this armour was well-known to the men.

197 Morti – Death personified as a god who had to be appeased with
sacrifices.

198–9 raptasque ... pecudes – probably 'flocks' rather than 'herds' as
oxen have already been mentioned.

199–201 litore toto – ablative of place. **semustaque servant busta** –
'and they keep watch over the half-burnt pyres'; *busta* are pyres that
have been set on fire.

201–2 donec – to be taken first. **invertit** – night is thought of as
'turning the sky round', because it was widely believed that there were
two hemispheres of sky, one bright for the daytime and one dark for
night-time. **aptum** – 'studded'.

203 et – 'also'. **nec minus ... miseri** – an example of litotes*.

205–6 virum = *virorum*. **terrae infodiunt** – 'they buried in the
ground'; inhumation was more common than cremation in early
Rome. By Virgil's day cremation was almost universal, but public
records survived from the fifth century BCE listing both cremation
and inhumation. In Homer's world cremation was the norm; here
perhaps Virgil wishes to emphasize the diversity of cultures that
he imagined must have existed in this early period. **avectaque partim
... tollunt** – 'and other (bodies) they carried away and removed'.
finitimos ... in agros – 'into neighbouring territories': i.e. the Latin
allies who had come from beyond the territory of Laurentum were
taken home for burial, if they were not cremated on the spot. **urbique
remittunt** – 'and (others) they sent back to the city', i.e. to Laurentum.

AS

207-8 cetera – supply *corpora*. **confusaeque ingentem caedis acervum** – 'a huge pile of dead all jumbled together'; the -*que* does not add a new idea but explains or amplifies *cetera*; *caedes* is used by Virgil to mean the victims of killing, as well as the abstract concept of slaughter. Note the heavy alliteration* of *c*-, here and in 209. **nec numero nec honore** – lit. 'with neither number nor honour'; the precise meaning of *numero* is unclear: it may mean 'without counting them' or 'without order'. These bodies are presumably those of rank and file soldiers, who did not merit special treatment.

208-9 vasti . . . agri – 'fields far and wide'. **certatim** – 'eagerly', in the sense that fire eagerly took hold of the timber of the pyres. Note the slow rhythm and heavy alliteration* of line 209. The wealth of detail and stylistic effects in the description of the burial rites may be interpreted as indicating Virgil's abhorrence of war.

210 tertia lux – 'the third dawn' (after the pyres were lit); they had to allow the embers to cool down before they could complete the burials.

211-12 ruebant – here transitive: 'raked up'. **focis** – 'on the pyres'. The bone fragments left over from the cremations were mixed in with the deep wood ash; the mourners used rakes to pull the bone fragments to the surface of the ash so that they could be collected. **tepido . . . aggere** – 'in a tepid mound'; the bones are still warm.

213-4 in tectis . . . urbe – 'in the buildings (in) the city'; the scene moves from the fields where the pyres were built to Latinus' city, where the families of the dead continued their mourning. **praecipuus fragor** – 'the loudest clamour' (of lamentation). **longi . . . luctus** – 'of the long period of mourning'.

215-17 hic . . . hic – the anaphora* moves the focus from one group of bereaved relatives to another. **cara sororum pectora maerentum** – 'the loving hearts of mourning sisters'; the switch of subject from people to part of the body breaks up what would otherwise be a routine list. Virgil lists all categories of bereaved relatives, apart from fathers, as his focus is on females, who were traditionally the principal mourners. **Turnique hymenaeos** – '(and they cursed) Turnus' wedding', i.e. the wedding he had planned with Lavinia, but which the arrival of Aeneas had threatened. Note the spondaic rhythm of 217.

218 ipsum armis ipsumque ... ferro – emphatic repetition of the same idea: each *ipsum* refers to Turnus.

219 regnum Italiae – not of course the whole of Italy, but that part of Italy which concerns the epic, i.e. Latium. **poscat** – the subjunctive either expresses cause ('because he was demanding') or is simply in a subordinate clause in indirect speech.

220–1 saevus Drances – Drances, the leader of the embassy to Aeneas to seek a truce, was described as *odiis et crimine infensus* in 122–3; *saevus* reminds us of his hostility towards Turnus. **solumque vocari testatur** – 'and testified that (Turnus) alone was being called out (to fight by Aeneas)', as made clear in the following amplification (*solum ... Turnum*).

222 multa ... contra ... sententia – supply *erat*: 'there was much contrary opinion (expressed)'. **variis dictis** – 'with a variety of arguments'.

223 magnum reginae nomen obumbrat – 'the great name of the queen defended him'. In Book VII Juno had infected queen Amata (the wife of Latinus) with a hatred of the Trojans and a longing to see Turnus become her son-in-law. Now the power of her name 'shelters' him.

224 multa fama – 'his great reputation', caused by the *meritis tropaeis* ('the trophies he had won'). **virum sustentat** – 'gave the man support'. The idea is that, the more enemies a hero killed in battle, the greater his heroic status.

AS

*225–497: Ambassadors have been sent by Latinus to Diomede, a Greek
hero from the Trojan War who has settled in South-east Italy, to ask for
help in fighting the Trojans. They return with a negative response.
Latinus summons a council of the leaders of his alliance and they listen
to Diomede's response, delivered by Venulus. Whereas the Latins have
hoped that Diomede, who had spent ten years fighting against the
Trojans at Troy, would wish to continue to oppose them in Italy, Diomede
in fact wants only peace. He laments the sufferings of the Greek leaders
after the conquest of Troy, which he sees as divine retribution for fighting
an unjust war. He praises the valour and honour of Aeneas, whom he
compares favourably with Hector, the greatest Trojan warrior during
the war. He advises the Latins to make peace.*

*Latinus now addresses the assembled council. He proposes that, since
war has achieved nothing, they should now offer peace to the Trojans,
granting them land on which to settle. Drances next speaks in support of
Latinus' proposal; he addresses Turnus and begs him either to abandon
his opposition to the Trojans and to Aeneas' marriage with Lavinia, or
to face Aeneas in single combat.*

*Turnus is angered by Drances' words and accuses him of cowardice.
He argues that the Trojans have lost just as many men as have the
Latins and their allies, and have by no means won the war. The
Latins also have further allies to call upon, including Camilla and
her Volscian army. There is therefore no reason to cease fighting
the Trojans. If, however, Aeneas wishes to meet him in single combat,
he will gladly accept the challenge; for he is second to none of the
great heroes of legend. Despite this bravado, he prefers pitched battle to
single combat, as, unlike Aeneas, he is fighting only to serve his own
interests.*

*At that moment the guards report that the Trojans and their Etruscan
allies are sweeping across the plain towards the city, ready for battle.
This angers the Latins and the younger men call for their arms, though
their parents fear for them.*

**A
Level**

Turnus takes charge and gives his battle orders. No one can stand in his way, and Latinus closes his council, regretting that he did not insist on welcoming Aeneas and his people when they first approached him. As the defenders man the walls and dig ditches in front of the gates, the womenfolk, including Amata and Lavinia, pray to Minerva, goddess of war, to give them victory; others climb onto the city walls to observe the impending battle.

Turnus dons his armour and hurries through the city towards the gates, resembling a stallion that exults in newly-found freedom.

498–521

Camilla runs to meet Turnus and offers to attack the Trojans. Turnus gratefully accepts; this will allow him to focus on setting an ambush to trap the Trojan infantry as they climb a mountain pass on the way to the city.

498–9 The order is *Camilla occurrit obvia cui, acie Volscorum comitante.* **cui** – Turnus. **Camilla** – she was the daughter of the king of the Volsci, a tribe living near the southern borders of Latium; raised as a warrior from childhood, she served the cult of Diana, the maiden goddess of hunting. Virgil models her on the Amazons, a race of warrior-maidens who lived, according to legend, on the fringes of the Greek world. The heavy alliteration* of *c-* draws attention to this first appearance of Camilla in the war.

499–501 regina – 'princess'; Virgil points out Camilla's high status, which makes her deference to Turnus (dismounting from her horse) all the more respectful. The same deference is shown by all her cavalrymen (*tota cohors*), who 'swept down' from their horses in imitation of her (*quam . . . imitata*). **relictis . . . equis** – ablative absolute: 'leaving their horses' (as they dismounted). **talia** – 'these words'.

A Level

502 The order is *si merito est forti qua fiducia sui*: 'if there is deservedly for a brave person any confidence in himself/herself', i.e. 'if a brave person deservedly has any confidence in himself/herself'. **sui** – objective genitive, dependent on *fiducia*. **est** – the use of *esse* + dative of a person is a regular way of expressing possession.

503 audeo – supply *occurrere*; the verb is made emphatic by its isolation at the start of the line and by the elision of the long -*o* before the short *et*. **promitto occurrere** – poetic for *promitto me occursuram esse*. **turmae** – dative dependent on the compound verb; a *turma* was a squadron of cavalry, and Camilla intends to use her own cavalry to attack that of the Trojans.

504 sola – 'alone' in the sense that the Volsci will carry out this attack alone, leaving Turnus and the rest of his allies free to make other arrangements to defend the city. This line largely repeats the promise made in the previous line.

505 me sine – 'allow me': Camilla defers to Turnus' leadership. **prima** – scanning the line will show that this adjective agrees with *pericula*, not *manu*; *prima* marks the fact that this will be her first foray into the war. **manu** – 'with my hand, i.e. 'in combat'.

506 pedes – nom.: 'as a foot-soldier'. **ad muros** – 'at the walls'.

507 oculos . . . fixus – 'with his eyes fixed'; see note on line 35 for the construction.

508–9 quas . . . parem – in full this would be *quas grates parem dicere, quasve grates parem referre*. **parem** – subjunctive in a deliberative question. **referre** – 'repay' (i.e. with deeds).

509–10 nunc – 'as it is'. **quando** – to be taken first. **est supra omnia** – 'is beyond all thanks'. **partire** – 'share' (imperative).

A Level

511–13 fidem . . . reportant – lit. 'bring back reliability', and so 'report reliably'. **improbus** – best here as an adverb: 'shamelessly'; this is no objective criticism of Aeneas' code of honour in sending forward troops, but a generic epithet that Turnus likes to apply to Aeneas. **equitum levia . . . arma** – 'light arms of cavalry', and so 'lightly-armed cavalry'. **quaterent** – jussive subjunctive, in an implied indirect command: 'with orders to . . .'; the verb has been variously interpreted as 'harass', 'scour', or 'reconnoitre', but its basic meaning is 'shake' and it is used elsewhere by Virgil to describe the drumming of hooves on the ground; perhaps 'trample' is a reasonable compromise.

513–14 ipse – supply 'Aeneas'. **ardua montis** – 'the high (parts) of the mountain'. **iugo** – 'by (way of) the ridge'.

515 furta . . . belli – lit. 'tricks of war', and so 'an ambush'. **silvae** – 'through the wood'.

516 bivias . . . fauces – either 'both ends of the pass' or 'the pass where it forks'.

517 Tyrrhenum equitem – singular for plural; the Etruscans were allied to the Trojans. **conlatis signis** – a military phrase meaning literally 'bring the standards together', i.e. 'take up position' (not as Gransden suggests 'join battle', as the perfect participle precludes this). **excipe** – another military word.

518–19 Messapus – a Latin cavalry commander often mentioned in this half of the *Aeneid*. **turmaeque Latinae** – supply *erunt tecum*. **Tiburti manus** – 'and the contingent of Tiburtus (will be with you)'; according to Book VII, Tiburtus was the son of the founder of the city of Tibur near Rome and brother of two Latin commanders. **ducis et tu concipe curam** – 'you also must take on the duty of (being) leader', i.e. along with me (or more likely along with Messapus and Tiburtus).

A Level

520–1 paribus . . . dictis – 'with similar words', i.e. he gave the same orders to Messapus, Tiburtus and the other leaders of the Latin cavalry. This suggests that they shared the command with Camilla, rather than being under her command.

522–31: Turnus sets up an ambush at the head of a valley that the Trojans must pass through on their way to Laurentum.

532–96

The goddess Diana addresses Opis, one of her handmaidens. In a digression (technically called an epyllion) she describes the childhood of Camilla and relates how the child was raised by her father Metabus to be her devotee. Now that Camilla is doomed to die, Diana orders Opis to take a bow and quiver of arrows and be ready to shoot dead any man who wounds Camilla.

532–5 interea – this marks a change of scene. **superis in sedibus** – 'in the dwellings of heaven'. **velocem . . . Opim** – a nymph and attendant of Diana; she is described as 'swift' to suggest that she too was a huntress. The subject is *Latonia* and the verb *compellabat*. **virginibus sociis sacraque caterva** – 'her sacred band of companion maidens' (hendiadys*); just as Diana remained a virgin, so did her companions. **ore dabat** – 'gave from her mouth' and so 'began to utter'.

536 nostris . . . armis – i.e. javelin, bow and arrows, as used in hunting. **nequiquam** – 'in vain' because she is fated to die. Note the enclosing word-order*.

537–8 novus iste Dianae venit amor – 'that love of Diana has (not) come new', and so 'that love which Diana has for her is no new phenomenon'. The force of *iste* has been variously interpreted, as

A Level

'which I have', 'that you know', 'that I have just mentioned'; all are questionable, since the usual use of the pronoun is to refer to the second person; a way round this is to suppose that for a moment Diana imagines herself addressing Camilla ('the love I have for you'); this may help to explain another difficulty: why Diana refers to herself in the third person (especially so soon after saying *mihi*). **subita** – conveys the same idea as *novus*.

539–40 The order is *cum Metabus, pulsus regno ob invidiam viresque superbas, excederet antiqua urbe, Priverno*. **ob invidiam . . . viresque superbas** – 'because of hatred of his arrogant strength' (hendiadys*). **Priverno** – Privernum was a Volscian town, 40 miles south-east of Rome. **Metabus** – Camilla's father; since he and Camilla do not feature in any earlier literature, they appear to be Virgil's invention; thus we have no details of his arrogant behaviour.

541–2 infantem . . . exsilio comitem – 'the baby (i.e. Camilla) as a companion for his exile'; *exsilio* is predicative dative. **belli** – presumably the war against Metabus and his supporters that drove him out.

542–3 mutata parte – 'after changing part (of the name)'. Virgil perhaps chose the name 'Camilla' because contemporaries would associate it with the noble Camilli family and because the name already existed referring to maidens associated with religious cults in Rome.

544–5 sinu – local ablative. **portans** – supply *eam*. **solorum** – 'lonely'.

546 volitabant . . . Volsci – 'the Volsci were charging back and forth', i.e. were hunting him from all sides.

547–9 fugae medio – 'in the middle of their flight' in the sense of 'blocking their flight'. **Amasenus** – a river near Privernum. **summis . . . ripis . . . abundans** – 'overflowing the tops of its banks'; the verb is intransitive, and so here the ablative takes the place of

A Level

an accusative. Note the enclosing word-order*. **se . . . ruperat** – 'had burst forth'.

550–1 secum versanti – supply *ei*: 'to him turning over in his mind'. **subito vix** – 'suddenly but reluctantly' (oxymoron*): it was a decision he quickly made, but one he did not wish to make because of the danger. **sedit** – 'became fixed (in his mind)'.

552–3 quod – to be taken before *manu valida*. **bellator** – i.e. Metabus. **solidum nodis et robore cocto** – 'solid with knots and seasoned oak'; knotty wood is very tough; timber was 'cooked' over a hearth to season it.

554–5 huic – 'to this (javelin)'; this leaves *telum* without any syntactical link to the rest of the sentence. **libro** – *liber* here has its basic meaning of 'bark' (used by early Romans to write upon, whence 'book'). **silvestri subere** – 'cork from the forest'; together the three words may be taken as an hendiadys*: 'the bark of cork-wood from the forest'. Metabus' use of cork was a double safety-measure: to keep the child from squirming as the javelin flew, and to help her to float if his throw fell short. **habilem** – 'so as to be manageable', i.e. not interfere with his throw. **hastae** – dative after the compound verb.

556 aethera – Greek accusative singular ending.

557–8 alma . . . nemorum cultrix – *alma* is either independent of *nemorum cultrix*, meaning 'o kind (goddess)', or defines *cultrix*: 'o caring custodian of the groves'; some take *cultrix* here to mean 'inhabitant'. **tibi hanc** – these two words, interrupting the naming and defining of the recipient of his prayer, should be taken with *famulam voveo*. **ipse pater** – *ipse* emphasizes his right as father to dispose of the child as he wishes. **hanc . . . famulam** – 'this child as (your) servant'. **voveo** – a strong vow that he cannot subsequently revoke.

A Level

558–9 tua prima ... tela – she holds 'your weapon first'; plural for singular, as there is only one javelin involved; Metabus now chooses to regard his javelin as a hunting spear (dedicated to Diana in 566) rather than a weapon of war (dedicated to Mars). **per auras** – to be taken with *fugit*. **fugit** – the scansion shows this to be present tense.

559–60 accipe ... tuam – supply *famulam*. **testor** – normally 'I bear witness', here it has the secondary meaning of 'I call upon (you) to witness'. **dubiis ... auris** – 'to the uncertain breezes'.

561–2 adducto ... lacerto – 'drawing back his arm'. **contortum hastile** – *contortum* is a difficult word to translate; the verb *contorqueo* is frequently used in poetry with two meanings: to brandish (a weapon), i.e. to balance it in the hand before throwing; and (more often) actually to cast the weapon. Here the phrase must mean 'the javelin that he had balanced', i.e. 'he balanced and (then) cast the javelin'. Most editors translate *contortum* as 'spinning' or 'whirling', which do not fit the participle. **immittit** – the enjambment* marks the sudden effort of discharge and the anticipation of the result.

562–3 sonuere undae – 'the waters roared', adding detail to enhance the vividness of the scene. **rapidum** – this, together with the asyndeton*, also brings the scene more to life. **infelix ... Camilla** – she is 'unfortunate' not because the attempt failed, but because of the danger involved; however, we shall not know she is safe until 566.

564–6 magna ... caterva – the enemies who are pursuing him. **victor** – 'victoriously'. **donum Triviae** – in apposition to *hastam*: 'a gift to Diana'; *Trivia* was an epithet of Diana, as goddess of crossroads.

567–8 The order is *non ullae urbes accepere illum tectis, non (ullae urbes illum accepere) moenibus*. **manus dedisset** – 'nor would he have surrendered'; the phrase *manus dare* means to offer the hands (to a victor or captor) to be bound; here it is generally interpreted figuratively to mean that Metabus would not have yielded to the offer of civilized life, though it could be taken literally, to mean that he would not have surrendered to his pursuers. **feritate** – 'because of his wildness' (causal ablative).

569 et – to be taken before *pastorum*. **pastorum . . . aevum** – he lived 'the life of shepherds', not 'the life of a shepherd': his life was like that of the shepherds, out on the 'lonely mountains'; he probably did not become a shepherd himself.

570–2 lustra – either dens of wild animals, full of bristles (as most take it) or woodland that is thorny. **armentalis equae** – a 'herd-mare', i.e. a 'brood mare' (used for breeding). **mammis et lacte ferino** – 'on wild milk from the teats' (hendiadys*). **immulgens ubera labris** – 'pressing its udders to her lips'.

573–4 – 'and when she had planted (*institerat*) the first footprints with the soles of her feet'; *primis* is hypallage*, transferred from *vestigia* to *plantis*.

575 parvae – 'of the little girl'.

576–7 pro crinali auro – 'instead of gold for her hair', i.e. 'instead of a gold headband'. **exuviae** – lit. 'things stripped off', and so here 'skin'. The skin covered her body and head.

578 iam tum – 'already'. **tela . . . puerilia** – 'child-sized weapons'. **torsit** – 'she has wielded'; the perfect tense, like *egit* and *deiecit*, is akin to the historic present, and so may be rendered 'she had wielded'.

579 fundam . . . egit – 'she whirled a sling'. **tereti . . . habena** – 'by a smooth thong'.

580 Strymoniam gruem – the cranes of the river Strymon in Thrace were famous; here it is simply a learned or ornamental epithet.

A Level

581–2 frustra – because she was devoted to the maiden goddess Diana. **Tyrrhena per oppida** – either they had wandered in their exile north of the Tiber into Etruria, or Virgil is assuming that Etruscan territory extended as far south as Volscian land at this early period; since it was Volscians rather than Etruscans that drove Metabus out and then hunted him, it is probably the former. **nurum** – predicative: 'as a daughter-in-law'.

582–4 sola contenta Diana – 'content with Diana alone' (as the scansion shows). Note the chiasmus* in 583 and enjambment* in 584.

584–5 vellem – 'I could have wished': imperfect subjunctive to express a wish in past time; the speaker is Diana, picking up from 537. **haud correpta fuisset** – 'that she had not become caught up in'; the 'double' pluperfect passive is best treated as equivalent to *correpta esset* (subjunctive in a past unfulfilled wish). **tali** – 'such as this', i.e. between the Trojans and Latins. **conata** – in full this would be *neve conata fuisset*: 'and that she had not tried'.

586 foret (= *esset*) – most editors take this to be a further wish: 'and that she were . . .'; however the asyndeton suggests that the subjunctive is expressing the apodosis of an unfulfilled condition: '(if only she had not got caught up in the war), she would now be . . .'. **cara mihi** – 'dear to me' would be illogical, as clearly Camilla is still dear to Diana; elsewhere (e.g. 215) Virgil uses the adjective with an active meaning; if it is used in this way here, the dative would be one of advantage and the meaning 'affectionate towards me' or 'loving of me'; the logic would be that, in turning from hunting to warfare, Camilla has abandoned Diana (and so she is no longer one of the goddess's companions).

587 verum age – marks the transition from digression to command. **urgetur** – the subject is Camilla.

588 labere – 'glide down' (imperative).

A Level

589 The order is *ubi tristis pugna committitur infausto omine.* Note the chiastic* order. **infausto ... omine** – Diana knows that Camilla is fated to die, a fate she cannot change.

590 haec – her own bow and arrows. **ultricem ... sagittam** – 'an arrow to avenge her'.

591–2 hac – supply *sagitta.* **violarit** = *violaverit* (future perfect indicative). **sacrum ... corpus** – Camilla's body is sacred because vowed to Diana. **Italusque** – 'or Italian'; *-que* is used to indicate that these are the Italian allies of the Trojans.

593–4 nube cava – 'in a hollow cloud'; in Greek mythology deities often wrapped themselves or others in a cloud or mist to conceal them. **inspoliata** – best taken with both *corpus* and *arma.* **tumulo** – dative of goal of motion (= *ad tumulum*; sim. *patriae*). **patriaeque reponam** – 'and restore (them) to her native land'.

595–6 illa – Opis. **delapsa** – 'as she sped down'. **circumdata ... corpus** – 'her body wrapped': Greek middle construction (see note on 35).

597–647: The cavalry of the Trojans and their allies approach Laurentum. The Latins and their allies ride to meet them. The battle ebbs and flows, with first one side and then the other achieving dominance. Finally, the two sides become locked together in combat, with neither side giving way.

648–89

Meanwhile, Camilla, supported by women-friends, fights and kills many on the Trojan side.

648–52 – See the Worked Example on the companion website for a stylistic analysis of these lines.

A Level

648–9 exsultat Amazon – 'the Amazon runs amok'; most editors translate *Amazon* as 'like an Amazon', but surely the word carries more force as a metaphor than as a simile? Then *Camilla*, deferred till the end of the second line, becomes a climax. Amazons supposedly cut off one breast so as not to hinder bowshots. **unum exserta latus** – 'with one side (i.e. breast) bared'; Greek middle construction – see note on 35). **pugnae** – dative of purpose.

650–1 lenta . . . hastilia – either 'tough' or 'flexible' javelins. **spargens . . . denset** – 'she hurls thick and fast'; this is hyperbole*, as there must have been a limit to the number of spears she could carry. Scan 651 to construe *dextra* and *indefessa*. Camilla's *aristeia* is introduced with the mention of three distinct weapons, indicating her versatility as a warrior.

652 aureus . . . arcus – the bow is 'golden' either because it is gilded or because it is made of gold-coloured wood; the adjective should be taken with both *arcus* and *arma*. **sonat** – Virgil is fond of referring to the sound effects of weapons, whether javelins or arrows, as they fly through the air.

653–4 in tergum – 'backwards'. **spicula . . . fugientia** – 'fleeing arrows', i.e. 'arrows as she fled' (hypallage*). **converso . . . arcu** – 'with her bow turned back'. In Virgil's day, the cavalry of Parthia (just beyond the eastern edge of the Roman empire and close to the traditional home of the Amazons) were famous for shooting backwards from their horses.

655–6 Larina . . . Tulla . . . Tarpeia – supply *erant*; these are all invented by Virgil, but they are given names that readers would associate with well-known places or people.

657–8 Italides – a word coined by Virgil. **decus sibi** – 'as a guard of honour for herself'. **bonas . . . ministras** – like *decus, ministras* is predicative: 'and to be her good attendants'.

A
Level

659–63 quales – introduces an epic simile* (in full *tales fuerunt quales*): 'they were like …'. **Threiciae … Amazones** – 'Thracian Amazons'; for the Greeks, Thrace represented the far North of their world, and that is Virgil's reason for using the name; in fact, the river Thermodon lay further east, flowing into the Black Sea and lying possibly within the territory associated with the Amazons. **flumina Thermodontis** – 'the river Thermodon'; *Thermodontis* gives a spondaic fifth foot (rare in Virgil). **cum … pulsant** – 'when they pound' the river with the hooves of their horses; Virgil imagines the river to be iced over; the present tense is used to suggest that the Amazons were still active in Virgil's day. **pictis … armis** – 'with painted arms': probably referring to their shields. **Hippolyten** – she and Penthesilea were the two most famous Amazon queens. **seu … refert** – the order is *seu cum Martia Penthesilea refert se curru*. **se … refert** – 'returns' from victorious battle. **ululante** – usually 'wailing' but here 'crying out with joy'. **feminea … agmina** – 'the army of women'. **lunatis … peltis** – the Amazons traditionally had crescent-shaped shields.

664–5 quem … quem … quot – rhetorical questions* addressed in apostrophe* to Camilla; they serve as a way of introducing the *aristeia* of Camilla now that her description is completed. **deicis … fundis** – the historic present tenses present Camilla's combats as if being acted out on the stage in front of the reader's eyes. **humi … fundis** – 'you strew on the ground'.

666–7 – None of the characters killed by Camilla has appeared previously. **Clytio … patre** – 'whose father was Clytius' (ablative absolute). **apertum … pectus** – '(whose) exposed breast'. **adversi** – 'as he faced her' (agreeing with *cuius*). **longa … abiete** – 'with her long pine spear'.

668–9 mandit humum – like our 'bites the dust'. **suo se in vulnere versat** – 'writhes around his wound'.

A
Level

670-1 Lirim Pagasumque – supply *transverberat* or similar. **super** – 'on top of him'. **quorum ... colligit** – the order is *quorum alter, revolutus suffuso equo dum colligit habenas*. **revolutus** – 'having rolled backwards (off his horse)'. **suffuso** – 'which had stumbled': an unusual use of the verb.

671-2 dextram . . . inermem – because he had to let go of his weapons to help his friend. **labenti** – 'to the falling man'.

675 This line contains two Greek accusatives.

676-7 quot . . . tot – 'as many (fell) as (the javelins she threw)'. **emissa** 'after releasing them'.

677-8 armis ignotis – 'with unfamiliar arms' (because he was a hunter rather than a warrior). **et** – joins two strange features of the man: he was riding (*fertur*) with unfamiliar arms and on an Iapygian horse.

679-80 cui – 'whose' (shoulders). **iuvenco pugnatori** – '(stripped) from a fighting (i.e. wild) bullock' (dative of disadvantage); some editors take *pugnatori* with *cui*, lit. 'to him as a fighter', i.e. 'when he became a fighter'; the word order allows both interpretations.

680-1 ingens oris hiatus et malae – 'the huge gape of the mouth and jaws (of a wolf)'; he had made the wolf's head into a helmet.

682-3 agrestis ... sparus – 'a rustic hunting-spear'. **vertitur** – 'he turned' (in retreat). **toto vertice supra est** – lit. 'is above with his whole head', i.e. 'he was a whole head taller than the rest'. His height and strange garb made him conspicuous.

684-5 hunc illa exceptum ... traicit – 'this man she intercepted and transfixed'. **labor** – supply *erat*: 'it was not difficult'. **agmine verso** – 'with the army in retreat'. **super** – '(standing) over him'. **haec** – supply *verba*.

A
Level

686 silvis – 'in the woods'. **putasti** = *putavisti*: 'did you think'.

687–8 The order is *dies advenit qui redargueret vestra verba muliebribus armis*. **qui . . . redargueret** – lit. 'which might refute', i.e. 'to refute'. **vestra . . . verba** – *vestra* refers to the boasts and taunts of the Etruscans generally.

688–9 nomen . . . haud leve . . . hoc – most editors take *nomen* to mean 'glory', i.e. the glory of having been killed by someone as famous as Camilla; an alternative interpretation is to take it literally: 'this is no insignificant name you will report: that you fell to the weapon of Camilla'. **patrum manibus** – 'to the shades of your forefathers', in the Underworld. Note the climactic position of *Camillae*.

690–724: Camilla continues her killing spree, even chasing after one fleeing man on foot and killing him.

725–835

Inspired by Jupiter, Tarchon, the Etruscan king and Trojan ally, rallies his fleeing troops and himself seizes Venulus and carries him away to kill him. While Camilla has her eyes fixed on the Trojan seer Chloreus, who was clad in purple and whose horse was decked with gold, the Etruscan Arruns pursues her unnoticed. When he hurls his javelin at her, he prays to Apollo to guide the weapon. Camilla is struck and, as she dies, she begs her friend Acca to hurry to Turnus and tell him that he is needed down on the plain to defend the city. Arruns flees.

725–6 non . . . nullis . . . oculis – lit. '(observing) not with no eyes', i.e. 'with watchful eyes' (litotes*). **altus** – 'high up'.

727–8 genitor – i.e. Jupiter. **stimulis haud mollibus** – litotes* again; we are not told how Jupiter did this.

A Level

729–31 cedentia agmina – 'the retreating armies'. **variis vocibus** – 'with various arguments'. **reficitque in proelia pulsos** – 'and gives the defeated men back the courage to return to the battle'.

732–3 o numquam dolituri – 'you men who will never feel shame'; that is, they will not be ashamed of being put to flight by a woman, as they should be. **inertes** – here perhaps 'spineless'. **animis** – dative: 'into your minds'.

734 palantes agit – 'drives you in disarray'. **vertit** – 'puts to flight'.

735 quo . . . quidve – 'to what purpose . . . or why'. **gerimus** – this verb has two objects: *ferrum* and *tela*.

736–7 at – making a strong contrast in his argument. **non segnes** – supply *estis*. **in Venerem** – 'to make love'. **nocturnaque bella** – 'nocturnal warfare', i.e. the activities of love. **choros . . . Bacchi** – 'Bacchic dances', i.e. wine-fuelled orgies.

738 exspectate – Tarchon now resorts to heavy sarcasm. **plenae . . . mensae** – '(cups set) on a loaded table' (genitive, perhaps of possession).

739–40 hic amor – supply *est*. **dum** – 'until', wherefore the subjunctive. **secundus haruspex** – lit. 'the propitious soothsayer': hypallage*, as the adjective logically defines *sacra*; translate 'propitiously'. The soothsayer's job was to oversee the sacrifice of an animal and then 'read' the omens from the internal organs. Once the sacrifice was declared propitious, i.e. the omens were good, the rest of the sacrificed animal was cooked and provided a feast for those attending. **hostia pinguis** – the fat was prized for the flavour it gave to the meat.

741–2 moriturus et ipse – 'ready to die himself too', rather than the more usual 'doomed to die', as there is no mention of his death subsequently; he is setting an example to his men. **in medios** – supply *hostes*. **Venulo adversum** – 'against Venulus'; *adversum* is an adjective

A Level

agreeing with *se*; Venulus was the Latin ambassador to Diomede (cf. 242). **turbidus** – 'violently'.

743–4 dextra – may be taken either with *dereptum* or *complectitur*. Tarchon sweeps Venulus onto his own horse. **concitus** – 'excitedly'.

746 convertēre = *convertērunt*.

746–7 igneus – 'swift as fire'. **aequore** – local ablative: 'across the plain'. **arma virumque** – Book I of the *Aeneid* opens with these words.

747–9 ipsius – i.e. of Venulus. **partes . . . apertas** – 'gaps in his armour'. **qua . . . ferat** – 'where he could deliver'.

749–50 sustinet – 'keeps . . . away' or 'blocks'; Tarchon is trying to stab him in the throat. **vim viribus exit** – 'wards off (Tarchon's) force with (his own) strength'; Page suggests 'seeks to evade force with force' to keep the play on words (polyptoton*), though the plural generally has a different meaning from the singular.

751–6 utque . . . cum – 'and just as when', introducing an epic simile*, with Tarchon compared to an eagle clutching a snake in its talons. **raptum . . . draconem** – 'a snake it has seized'. **implicuitque pedes atque unguibus haesit** – 'and has wrapped its feet (round it) and clung (to it) with its talons'; note the chiastic* word order. **at** – to be taken before *saucius*. Note the heavy alliteration* of 753. **arrectis horret squamis** – 'and bristles with raised scales'; Virgil was clearly unfamiliar with snakes, despite his fondness for using them in his writing: snakes cannot raise their scales. **arduus insurgens** – 'raising its head on high', to try to bite the eagle. **luctantem** – 'the snake as it struggles'.

757–8 haud aliter – the regular formula for returning to the person or thing being illustrated by the simile: 'in the same way'. **Tiburtum ex**

A Level

agmine – 'from the ranks of the Tiburtians'; the men of Tibur were allies of Latinus.

758–9 Maeonidae – the Etruscans, who were supposed to have originated in Asia Minor, of which Maeonia was a part; one of Virgil's 'ornate' references.

759–61 fatis debitus Arruns – 'Arruns owed to fate' i.e. 'destined to die'; he will kill Camilla and so be killed in turn by Opis, as Diana had decreed (591–2); Arruns has not appeared elsewhere. The order is *tum Arruns, debitus fatis, prior circuit velocem Camillam iaculo et multa arte.* **prior** – variously interpreted as 'first', 'superior in cunning', 'anticipating her movements', 'keeping one step ahead'. **fortuna** – 'opportunity' (to strike). **temptat** – 'tries to determine'.

762 qua . . . cumque – the single word *quacumque* has been split in two (a feature called *tmesis*): **se . . . tulit** – 'bore herself' and so 'dashed'.

763 hac – neatly counterbalances *qua*: 'here'.

764–5 qua . . . hac – 'where . . . here', repeating the balanced phrase. **pedem reportat** 'retires'. **celeres detorquet habenas** – to turn the horse round; the reins are 'swift' because Arruns is using them to make the horse move quickly (hypallage*).

766–7 hos aditus iamque hos aditus . . . pererrat – 'he tries (now) one approach and now another'. **omnemque pererrat undique circuitum** – 'and circles all round her'. **pererrat** – a difficult word, here used with two distinct objects (*aditus* and *circuitum*), requiring a different meaning for each phrase (zeugma*); its basic meaning is 'wander through', which fits neither context literally. **improbus** – 'wicked' because he is going to kill a person of heroic virtue in a sly manner (cf. 512).

768 sacer Cybelo – 'sacred to Mt Cybelus'; Cybelus was a mountain in Phrygia in Asia Minor that was the centre of the cult of Cybele; here

A Level

the name of the mountain stands for that of the goddess. **olimque sacerdos** – i.e. before he left Troy.

770–1 The order is ... *equum, quem pellis tegebat, aenis squamis in plumam, conserta auro.* **in plumam** – 'like feathers': the bronze scales overlapped like a series of feathers. **conserta auro** – if taken literally, this means that threads of gold were woven into the hide; probably these threads were used to fasten the bronze scales to the hide. The important thing is that this horse stood out from the rest, being so richly caparisoned.

772–3 peregrina ferrugine clarus – 'resplendent with exotic brown'; *ferrugo* is literally 'rust-colour', but appears to cover a wider range of colours. **spicula ... Gortynia** – 'Cretan arrows'; Gortys was a large city on Crete. **Lycio ... cornu** – 'from his Lycian bow'; Lycia was a province of Asia Minor; both adjectives are 'ornate' epithets, of which Virgil and other poets were fond, and they are used to make Chloreus appear more exotic and rich; both places were associated with archery.

774–5 aureus ... arcus – 'a gilded bow'. **ex umeris** – was suspended (*erat*) from his shoulders'; this suggests that *torquebat* in 773 does not mean that Chloreus was at that moment shooting Cretan arrows, but that the arrows he had for shooting were Cretan.

775–6 tum ... -que – 'then too' (-*que* needs to be brought forward). **sinusque crepantes carbaseos** – 'with its rustling, fine linen folds' (lit. 'cloak and its folds', a sort of hendiadys*).

777 pictus acu –this is the Greek middle construction (cf. 35 note) and should be translated 'and his tunic ... were embroidered'. **barbara tegmina crurum** – lit. 'the barbarous coverings of his legs', and so 'his foreign trousers'; Phrygian men traditionally wore trousers, which were viewed with contempt by the Romans.

A Level

778–82 hunc virgo – the syntax is interrupted by two alternative *ut* clauses, resuming at *hunc*. The order for this main clause is *caeca virgo sequebatur hunc unum ex omni certamine pugnae*. **templis praefigeret** – the hanging by triumphant victors of captured arms outside a temple was common practice in Roman times. **arma Troia** – 'arms from Troy' (ablative of origin). **sive ut se ferret** – 'or to display herself'. **venatrix** – 'as a huntress', i.e. 'when she went hunting'; Page places the comma before *venatrix*, to link the word to her pursuit of Chloreus, which perhaps gives better sense. **caeca ... incauta** – because she ignored threats to herself. **femineo ... ardebat amore** – 'she was inflamed with a woman's desire' for the booty; since women were not in the habit of seeking or taking plunder on the battlefield, Virgil is probably thinking of the nature of this specific plunder: gold and fine decoration. **praedae et spoliorum** – the same thing; the tautology makes Camilla's lust for possession appear stronger.

783–4 The subject now switches to Arruns. The order is *cum tandem Arruns, tempore capto, concitat telum ex insidiis et precatur superos sic voce*. **cum** – this is the 'inverse *cum*' construction, with the indicative. **ex insidiis** – not strictly 'from an ambush', because that would have required him to wait in one place for his enemy to appear; Williams suggests 'from where he was lurking'. **tempore capto** – 'seizing his chance'. **Arruns** – note how Virgil builds suspense by holding the name back, making us think it is Camilla that has hurled the javelin at Chloreus. **voce** – 'out loud'.

785 deum = *deorum*. **sancti custos Soractis** – Apollo had a temple on the summit of Mt Soracte (near Rome in southern Etruria); priests of the cult practiced fire-walking.

786–8 quem primi colimus – 'whom we first worship' and so 'whose principal worshippers we are'. **cui** – 'in whose honour'. **pineus ardor**

acervo pascitur – lit. 'pine-wood heat is nourished in a heap', i.e. 'a heap of burning pine-wood is tended' (for the priests to walk upon). **cultores** – 'we worhippers'. **multa pruna** – 'on a deep bed of burning coals'. These lines serve as the prelude to his prayer, identifying the deity and the relationship of the supplicant to the deity; such a preamble was customary in prayers.

789-90 da – 'grant': the usual word for a request to a deity. **pater . . . omnipotens** – a title usually reserved for Jupiter; here Arruns is showing that he places his deity even above Jupiter. **hoc . . . dedecus** – 'this dishonour', i.e. of so many allied men being killed by a woman. **nostris . . . armis** – 'by my weapons'.

790-2 exuvias . . . tropaeum . . . spolia – all related symbols of victory: 'spoils' stripped from the body, a 'trophy' set up using these spoils (like the one described in 5ff.), and more general 'plunder'. **cetera . . . facta** – 'the rest of my deeds' in the war.

792-3 dum – 'as long as' or 'provided that'. **haec dira . . . pestis** – a very strong term of abuse, heightened by the position of *pestis* and the alliteration* of *p-*. **inglorius** – i.e. without the glory of this particular victory.

794-5 dedit – 'granted' (cf. 789). **mente** – 'in his decision'. **volucres dispersit in auras** – 'he scattered on the swift breezes'; a frequent metaphor for rejection, here of the second part of Arruns' prayer, i.e. that he should return home.

796-7 The order is *adnuit oranti ut sterneret turbatam Camillam subita morte*. **oranti** – 'to the praying man'. **turbatam** – 'distracted' (by her pursuit of Chloreus).

797-8 ut patria alta videret – 'that his lofty fatherland should see him'; *alta* refers to the height of Mt Soracte. **vertere** = *verterunt*, as the scansion shows. **in Notos** – *Notus* is strictly speaking the South Wind;

A
Level

here the plural suggests winds in general. **procellae** – these are 'strong winds'; these words extend the metaphor of 795, the idea being that the winds take the words of the prayer and scatter them amongst themselves. The metaphor can be visualized better if it is remembered that in mythology the winds are portrayed as sentient beings, capable of obeying the commands of a god.

799 sonitum dedit – cf. 652 note.

800–1 convertere = *converterunt*, as in 798; the subject is *Volsci*. **animos acres** – 'their attention keenly'. Note the chiasmus* in 800. **Volsci** – deferred until the end to raise suspense: the irony is that every Volscian was aware of the javelin cast except for its target.

801–2 ipsa – in contrast with the rest of the Volsci. **aurae** – 'of the movement through the air'. **memor** – supply *fuit*. **aut** – used as a variation for *nec*.

803–4 donec – to be taken first. **perlata** – 'reaching all the way'. **haesit** – the enjambment* heavily emphasizes the fact that the javelin stayed fixed under the breast. **alte … acta** – 'driven deep'. **bibit cruorem** – a strong metaphor*.

805 ruentem – 'as she fell'.

806–8 exterritus – as this governs both *laetitia* and *metu*, it must mean 'dazed' rather than the literal 'terrified'. **nec iam amplius** – 'and no longer'. **telis occurrere virginis** – since Camilla was dying, it was highly unlikely that she would be able to retaliate; the point is that Arruns did not stop to see whether he had inflicted a mortal wound; Camilla's awesome reputation was enough to make him flee.

809–813 ac velut – another formula for introducing an epic simile*. **ille** – anticipates *lupus*, to be translated as 'the wolf' rather than 'a wolf'. **sequantur** – subjunctive of purpose. **sese … abdidit** – 'has

A Level

gone into hiding'; *abdidit* and *subiecit* may be considered so-called gnomic perfects (used to express general truths), in which case they may be translated as present tenses. **conscius audacis facti** – this gives the reason for the wolf's flight, and is parallel to Arruns' awareness of the magnitude of his act. **subiecit . . . utero** – 'has stuck (its tail) under its belly'; *utero* is dative after the compound verb. **pavitantem** – the tail is 'trembling' with fear. **silvasque petivit** – perhaps a rather weak ending to the simile, as the wolf has already hidden up in the mountains. The perfect tenses are all primary sequence to establish what the wolf has done (or alternatively gnomic perfects).

814–15 haud secus – cf. *haud aliter* (757 note). **turbidus** – 'frantically' (cf. 742 note). **contentusque fuga** – he has no desire to stay and plunder the body of Camilla.

816–17 ossa . . . mucro – the order is *sed ferreus mucro stat inter ossa ad costas alto vulnere* (*sed* and *inter* are postponed). Note the double alliteration*. **stat** – this verb is qualified by three adverbial phrases, all giving the spearhead's location: *inter ossa* ('between the (rib) bones'); *ad costas* ('by her ribs'); *alto vulnere* ('in a deep wound').

818–19 Note the alliteration* again, and the polyptoton* of *labitur / labuntur* (here 'drooping'). **frigida leto lumina** – 'her eyes, cold in death' (causal ablative).

820–2 sic – to be taken with *adloquitur*. **Accam . . . unam** – 'Acca alone'; she is not mentioned elsewhere. **fida . . . Camillae** – the order is *quae (erat) sola ante alias fida Camillae*. **ante alias . . . sola** – this does not mean that Acca was the only one faithful to Camilla, but that she was loyal far above the rest. **quicum** – this is an archaic form of *quacum*: 'with whom'. **partiri** – 'she (Camilla) used to share' (a sort of historic infinitive).

**A
Level**

823–4 hactenus . . . potui – 'until now I have been able' (to keep the Trojans at bay). **Acca soror** – not meant literally. **conficit** – supply *me*. **tenebris** – 'in darkness'.

825 novissima – poignant: her 'last' instructions.

826 succedat – 'let him take over' command of the battle. At the time Turnus was lying in ambush to catch the main infantry body of the Trojan army as it marched to Laurentum; now he was needed to save the city from the more immediate threat of the Trojan cavalry, which it had been Camilla's job to keep at bay.

827–8 simul his dictis – 'as soon as she had spoken these words'. **non sponte** – 'against her will' (litotes*).

828–31 toto paulatim exsolvit se corpore – 'slowly she withdrew from the whole of her body'; the idea is that on death the soul has to disentangle itself from the whole body, throughout which it is diffused. **captum leto** – 'overcome by death'. **indignata** – 'complaining', because of her untimely death. **sub umbras** – 'down to the Shades' (of the Underworld).

832–3 ferit aurea . . . sidera – 'struck the golden stars' (hyperbole*). Line 833 needs to be scanned to determine the cases of the three words ending in -*a*. **crudescit** – 'took a turn for the worse'.

834–5 densi – masculine plural to agree with all the men included in the *copia* and the *alae*, and also the *duces*. **Euandrique Arcades alae** – 'and the Arcadian squadrons of Evander'.

836–915: Opis, watching the battle round Camilla from a mountain top, sighs in lamentation when she sees Camilla fall. She promises Camilla fame and vengeance. Flying down, she lies in wait for Arruns. When she sees him, she shoots him dead with an arrow; he falls unnoticed by his fellows. The Latins, lacking the leadership of Camilla, are routed and flee

A Level

back to Laurentum, where there is chaos and bloodshed as the gates are closed, after some Trojans have managed to get inside, while many Latins are shut out and are at the mercy of the Trojans. Meanwhile Turnus receives the bad news from Acca and abandons his ambush. Soon after he begins his withdrawal to the city, Aeneas and the rest of his men climb through the pass. Nightfall puts an end to hostilities.

A
Level

Vocabulary

An asterisk * denotes a word in OCR's Defined Vocabulary List for AS.

*a, ab + *abl.*	from, away from, by
abdo, abdere, abdidi, abditum	to hide
abies, -etis *f.*	pine, fir
aboleo, abolere, abolevi, aboletum	to abolish, destroy
*absum, abesse, afui	to be absent
abundo, abundare, abundavi, abundatum	to overflow
*ac	and
Acca, -ae *f.*	Acca
accendo, accendere, accendi, accensum	to light
*accipio, accipere, accepi, acceptum	to accept, receive
*acer -cris -cre	keen, fierce
acerbus -a -um	bitter
acervus, -i *m.*	heap, pile
Acheron, -ntis *m.*	Acheron (Underworld river)
*acies, -ei *f.*	battle line, army
Acoetes, -is *m.*	Acoetes
acus, -us *f.*	needle
acutus -a -um	sharp
*ad + *acc.*	to, at
*addo, addere, addidi, additum	to add
adduco, adducere, adduxi, adductum	to draw back
*adhuc (*adv.*)	yet

aditus, -us *m.*	approach
adloquor, adloqui, adlocutus sum	to address
adnuo, adnuere, adnui, adnutum	to nod, assent
***adsum, adesse, adfui**	to be present
***advenio, advenire, adveni, adventum**	to arrive
advento, adventare, adventavi, adventatum	to advance rapidly, approach quickly
***adversus -a -um**	facing, opposite
Aeneades, -um *m.pl.*	the people of Aeneas, the Trojans
Aeneas, Aeneae *m.*	Aeneas
aënus -a -um	made of bronze
aequalis -e	equal, of the same age
aequo, aequare, aequavi, aequatum	to make equal
aequor, -oris *n.*	plain
***aequus -a -um**	equal, fair
aeratus -a -um	made of bronze
aes, aeris *n.*	bronze
aetas, -atis *f.*	age
aeternus -a -um	eternal, for ever
aether, -eris *m.*	sky, upper world, air
Aethon, -onis *m.*	Aethon
aevum, -i *n.*	age, old age, life
***ager, agri** *m.*	field, land, territory
agger, -eris *m.*	mound
aggero, aggerare, aggeravi, aggeratum	to pile up
agito, agitare, agitavi, agitatum	to chase, spur on
***agmen, -inis** *n.*	army, line of troops

*ago, agere, egi, actum	to drive, do, move, thrust, whirl;
age!	come now!
agrestis -e	rustic
aio (*defective verb*)	to say
ala, alae *f.*	wing, squadron (of cavalry)
albus -a -um	white
aliter (*adv.*)	otherwise, differently
*alius -a -ud	other, some
almus -a -um	restorative, nourishing, kindly
alo, alere, alui, alitum	to nourish
altaria, -ium *n.pl.*	altar(s)
*alter -era -erum	the one, the other (of two)
*altus -a -um	high, tall, deep
alumnus, -i *m.*	ward
Amasenus, -i *m.*	(river) Amasenus
Amastrus, -i *m.*	Amastrus
Amazon, -onis *f.*	Amazon
amictus, -us *m.*	garment
*amicus, -i *m.*	friend
amnis, -is *m.*	river
*amor, -oris *m.*	love
amplius (*adv.*)	more, further, longer
anima, -ae *f.*	soul, spirit
*animus, -i *m.*	mind, courage
*annus, -i *m.*	year
ante (*adv.*)	before, previously
*ante + *acc.*	before, in front of
antiquus -a -um	ancient
apertus -a -um	open, exposed
apparo, apparare, apparavi, apparatum	to prepare
apto, aptare, aptavi, aptatum	to fit

aptus -a -um	fitted, studded (with)
*aquila, -ae *f.*	eagle
arbuteus -a -um	of the strawberry-tree
Arcades, -um *m.pl.*	Arcadians (i.e. the people of Evander)
arceo, arcere, arcui, arctum	to keep … away
arcus, -us *m.*	bow
ardeo, ardere, arsi, arsum	to burn, be on fire
ardor, -oris *m.*	heat
arduus -a -um	steep, high
arguo, arguere, argui, argutum	to blame
*arma, -orum *n.pl.*	arms, weapons
armentalis -e	belonging to a herd
armiger, -eri *m.*	armour-bearer
armo, armare, armavi, armatum	to arm
arrigo, arrigere, arrexi, arrectum	to raise
Arruns, -ntis *m.*	Arruns
*ars, artis *f.*	skill
asper -era -erum	harsh, violent
aspernor, aspernari, aspernatus sum	to refuse, reject
aspicio, aspicere, aspexi, aspectum	to see, look upon
*at	but
ater, atra, atrum	black, dark
atque	and
attollo, attollere	to raise up
*audax, -acis	bold
*audeo, audere, ausus sum	to dare
*aufero, auferre, abstuli, ablatum	to steal, take away

aura, -ae *f.*	breeze, air
aureus -a -um	made of gold, golden, gilded
Aurora, -ae *f.*	Dawn
aurum, -i *n.*	gold
Ausonia, -ae *f.*	Ausonia, Southern Italy
Ausonius -a -um	Ausonian, Italian
auspicium, -i *n.*	auspices, omen
***aut**	or, either
aveho, avehere, avexi, avectum	to carry away
avello, avellere, avelli, avulsum	to pull away
avius -a -um	off the beaten track
Bacchus, -i *m.*	Bacchus (god of wine)
barbarus -a -um	barbarous, foreign
bellator, -oris *m.*	warrior, fighter
bellipotens, -ntis	mighty in war; as noun *m.* Mars
bellor, bellari, bellatus sum	to fight
***bellum, -i** *n.*	war
bipennis, -is *f.*	two-edged axe, battle axe
***bis**	twice
bivius -a -um	having two ways, forking
***bonus -a -um**	good
bos, bovis *m.*	ox
bustum, -i *n.*	lit pyre
***cado, cadere, cecĭdi, casum**	to fall
caecus -a -um	blind
***caedes, -is** *f.*	slaughter, bloodshed, the slain
caedo, caedere, cecīdi, caesum	to kill, cut down
caelestes, -ium *m.pl.*	heavenly gods
***caelum, -i** *n.*	sky, heaven
caespes, -itis *m.*	sod, turf

caligo, -inis *f.*	gloom, mist, darkness
Camilla, -ae *f.*	Camilla
*****campus, -i** *m.*	plain
*****capio, capere, cepi, captum**	to capture, take, catch, take in, seize
*****captivus -a -um**	captive, captured
*****caput, -itis** *n.*	head
carbaseus -a -um	of fine linen
*****carus -a -um**	dear, loving
Casmilla, -ae *f.*	Casmilla
cassida, -ae *f.*	metal helmet
cassus -a -um + *abl.*	deprived of
*****castra, -orum** *n. pl.*	camp
caterva, -ae *f.*	crowd, band
cauda, -ae *f.*	tail
*****causa, -ae** *f.*	cause, reason
cautus -a -um	cautious
cavus -a -um	hollow
*****cedo, cedere, cessi, cessum**	to retreat
cedrus, -i *f.*	cedar-tree
*****celer -eris -ere**	swift
*****certamen, -inis** *n.*	struggle, contest
certatim (*adv.*)	eagerly
*****certus -a -um**	certain, sure
cesso, cessare, cessavi, cessatum	to cease
*****ceteri -ae -a**	the rest, the other
chlamys, -ydis *f.*	Greek military cloak
Chloreus, -i *m.*	Chloreus
chorus, -i *m.*	dance
Chromis, -is (*acc.* **-im**), *m.*	Chromis
*****cingo, cingere, cinxi, cinctum**	to surround, gird
cinis, -eris *m.*	ashes
*****circa** (*adv.*)	round about, in the vicinity

circueo, circuire, circuii, circuitum	to circle round
circuitus, -us *m.*	circuit, way round
circum (*adv.*)	around
*circum + *acc.*	around, round
circumdo, circumdare, circumdedi, circumdatum	to surround
circumfundo, circumfundere, circumfudi, circumfusum	to surround
circumligo, circumligare, circumligavi, circumligatum	to tie to
*civis, -is *m.*	citizen
*clamor, -oris *m.*	shout, cry
clangor, -oris *m.*	strident sound
*clarus -a -um	bright, resplendent
claudo, claudere, clausi, clausum	to close, enclose, wrap
clipeus, -i *m.*	shield
Clytius, -i *m.*	Clytius
*cohors, -rtis *f.*	cohort, company of troops
colligo, colligere, collegi, collectum	to collect, gather
collum, -i *n.*	neck
*colo, colere, colui, cultum	to cultivate, cherish, worship
color, -oris *m.*	colour
comae, -arum *f.pl.*	hair
*comes, -itis *m/f.*	companion
comitor, comitari, comitatus sum	to accompany
*committo, committere, commisi, commissum	to commit, entrust, join (battle)
compello, compellare, compellavi, compellatum	to address

complector, complecti, complexus sum	to embrace
concedo, concedere, concessi, concessum	to grant
concieo, conciere, concivi, concitum	to excite
concipio, concipere, concepi, conceptum	to take on
concito, concitare, concitavi, concitatum	to spur on, hurl
concurro, concurrere, concurri, concursum	to meet, join battle, rush together
***condo, condere, condidi, conditum**	to plunge
***confero, conferre, contuli, conlatum**	to bring together
***conficio, conficere, confeci, confectum**	to wear out, destroy
confundo, confundere, confudi, confusum	to confuse, jumble together
conicio, conicere, conieci, coniectum	to throw, throw together
coniunx, -iugis *f.	wife
conluceo, conlucere	to shine brightly
***conor, conari, conatus sum**	to try
conscius -a -um	conscious, aware
consero, conserere, conserui, consertum	to join together, weave together
***constituo, constituere, constitui, constitutum**	to decide, construct
contentus -a -um	content
continuo (*adv.*)	immediately

contorqueo, contorquere, contorsi, contorsum	to brandish, balance, throw, cast
contra (*adv.*)	in the opposite direction, to meet them, on the other hand
***contra** + acc.*	against
converto, convertere, converti, conversum	to turn round, draw back, turn
convexus -a -um	arched
***copia, -ae** f.*	multitude, forces
coquo, coquere, coxi, coctum	to cook, season
cornu, -us *n.*	horn, bow
***corpus, -oris** n.*	body
***corripio, corripere, corripui, correptum**	to seize
costa, -ae *f.*	rib
cratis, -is *f.*	wickerwork
creber -bra -brum	crowded, numerous
***credo, credere, credidi, creditum**	to trust, believe, entrust
cremo, cremare, cremavi, crematum	to cremate
crepo, crepare, crepui, crepitum	to rustle
***crimen, -inis** n.*	crime, charge, accusation
crinalis -e	for the hair
crinis, -is *m.*	hair
crista, -ae *f.*	plume, crest
croceus -a -um	saffron, yellow
***crudelis -e**	cruel
crudesco, crudescere, crudui	to grow worse
cruentus -a -um	blood-soaked
cruor, -oris *m.*	blood
crus, cruris *n.*	leg

cultor, -oris *m.*	worshipper
cultrix, -icis *f.*	custodian
***cum**	when, since, although
***cum** + *abl.*	with
cumulo, cumulare, cumulavi, cumulatum	to pile up, heap up
***cuncti -ae -a**	all
cuneus, -i *m.*	wedge
***cura, -ae** *f.*	care, anxiety, trouble, responsibility, duty
currus, -us *m.*	chariot
curvus -a -um	curved
cuspis, -idis *f.*	javelin, spear-point
***custos, -odis** *m.*	guard, custodian
Cybelus, -i *m.*	(Mt.) Cybelus
daps, dapis *f.*	feast
***de** + *abl.*	about, from, down from, according to
***debeo, debere, debui, debitum**	to owe
decerno, decernere, decrevi, decretum	to fight it out, decide the issue
decet, decere, decuit (*impersonal*)	it is right, proper
decido, decidere, decidi, decisum	to cut off
decoro, decorare, decoravi, decoratum	to honour
decorus -a -um	decorated, ornate
decurro, decurrere, decurri, decursum	to march in procession
decus, -oris *n.*	honour, glory
dedecus, -oris *n.*	disgrace, dishonour
defleo, deflere, deflevi, defletum	to weep over

defluo, defluere, defluxi, defluxum	to flow down, sweep down
defringo, defringere, defregi, defractum	to break off
deicio, deicere, deieci, deiectum	to shoot down, kill
delabor, delabi, delapsus sum	to glide down
deligo, deligere, delegi, delectum	to choose, select
demeto, demetere, demessui, demessum	to cut off, pluck
Demophoon, -ontis (*acc.* **-onta**) *m.*	Demophoon
demoror, demorari, demoratus sum	to detain, delay
dens, -ntis *m.*	tooth
denseo, densere, –, densetum	to make thick, thicken
densus -a -um	in massed ranks
depromo, depromere, deprompsi, depromptum	to pull out, draw out
derigo, derigere, deregi, derectum	to aim, direct
deripio, deripere, deripui, dereptum	to strip, tear off, pull off
deserta, -orum *n.pl.*	uninhabited places, wasteland
desilio, desilire, desilui, desultum	to jump down
detorqueo, detorquere, detorsi, detortum	to turn aside
***deus, -i** *m.*	god, deity
***dext(e)ra, -ae** *f.*	right hand, hand
Diana, -ae *f.*	Diana
dictum, -i *n.*	word, argument

Dido, Didonis *f.*	Dido
***dies, diei** m.* or *f.*	day
dignor, dignari, dignatus sum	to think worthy
dimoveo, dimovere, dimovi, dimotum	to move aside, displace
***dirus -a -um**	dreadful
***discedo, discedere, discessi, discessum**	to depart, leave
discerno, discernere, discrevi, discretum	to interweave
discrimino, discriminare, discriminavi, discriminatum	to distinguish
dispergo, dispergere, dispersi, dispersum	to scatter
dius -a -um	godlike
diva, -ae *f.*	goddess
diversus -a -um	different
***do, dare, dedi, datum**	to give, grant
***doleo, dolere, dolui, dolitum**	to be sorry, be ashamed
***dolor, -oris** m.*	grief
domina, -ae *f.*	mistress
***domus, -us** f.*	house, home
donec	until
***donum, -i** n.*	gift
dorsum, -i *n.*	back
draco, -onis *m.*	snake
Drances, -is *m.*	Drances
***dubius -a -um**	doubtful, uncertain
***duco, ducere, duxi, ductum**	to lead, bring
dulcedo, -inis *f.*	sweetness, tenderness
***dum**	while, until, provided that; (after *nec*) yet

dumus, -i *m.*	thorn-bush
*durus -a -um	hard, tough
*dux, ducis *m.*	leader
*e(x) + *abl.*	out of, from
eburnus -a -um	ivory
ecce	behold, see, lo
educo, educere, eduxi, eductum	to lead out
effero, efferre, extuli, elatum	to bring out
*efficio, efficere, effeci, effectum	to accomplish, achieve
effor, effari, effatus sum	to speak
*effugio, effugere, effugi	to escape
*egeo, egere, egui + *gen.*	to lack
*ego, mei	I
egregius -a -um	distinguished, illustrious
eminus (*adv.*)	from a distance
emitto, emittere, emisi, **emissum**	to throw, release
*enim	for
ensis, -is *m.*	sword
*eo, ire, i(v)i, itum	to go
Eous, -i *m.*	Eous, the Morning Star
equa, -ae *f.*	mare
*eques, -itis *m.*	horseman, cavalryman; (pl.) cavalry
equidem	I for my part
*equus, -i *m.*	horse
*ergo (*adv.*)	therefore
eripio, eripere, eripui, ereptum	to strip, pull off
*erro, errare, erravi, erratum	to wander
*et	and, also, even
*etiam (*adv.*)	also, even

Euander, -ri *m.*	Evander
eum (*acc. of* *is*)	him
Eunaeus, -i *m.*	Eunaeus
eventum, -i *n.*	result, experience
everto, evertere, everti, eversum	to overturn, cast down
exanimus -a -um	lifeless, dead
exaudio, exaudire, exaudivi, exauditum	to listen to, heed
excedo, excedere, excessi, excessum	to leave
***excipio, excipere, excepi, exceptum**	to intercept
***exemplum, -i** *n.*	example
exeo, exire, exii, exitum	to go out, ward off, avoid
***exercitus, -us** *m.*	army
exigo, exigere, exegi, exactum	to pass, spend
exiguus -a -um	small, meagre
explorator, -oris *m.*	scout
exsanguis -e	bloodless, pale
exsecror, exsecrari, exsecratus sum	to curse
exsertus -a -um	bared, uncovered
***exsilium, -i** *n.*	exile
exsolvo, exsolvere, exsolvi, exsolutum	to release, separate
***exspecto, exspectare, exspectavi, exspectatum**	to expect, wait for
exspiro, exspirare, exspiravi, exspiratum	to expire
exstruo, exstruere, exstruxi, exstructum	to construct, build up

exsulto, exsultare, exsultavi, exsultatum	to exult, run amok
exterritus -a -um	terrified, dazed
exuviae, -arum *f.pl.*	spoils
***facilis -e**	easy
***facio, facere, feci, factum**	to make, do
factum, -i *n.*	deed, achievement
***fama, -ae** *f.*	fame, glory, reputation, rumour
famula, -ae *f.*	servant, attendant
famulus, -i *m.*	servant, attendant
fas (indecl.) *n.*	right (i.e. what is lawful)
fatalis -e	fatal, deadly, fated
fatum, -i *n.*	fate (also personified)
fauces, -ium *f.*	pass, defile
fax, facis *f.*	torch
***felix, -icis**	fortunate, favourable
***femina, -ae** *f.*	woman
femineus -a -um	female, of women, womanly
fera, -ae *f.*	wild beast
feretrum, -i *n.*	bier
ferinus -a -um	wild, from wild animals
ferio, ferire	to strike
feritas, -atis *f.*	wildness
***fero, ferre, tuli, latum**	to bear, carry, bring
ferreus -a -um	made of iron
ferrugo, -inis *f.*	rust-colour, brown
***ferrum, -i** *n.*	iron, sword
fervens, -ntis	red-hot
***fides, -ei** *f.*	faith, pledge, trust, loyalty, reliability
fiducia, -ae *f.*	confidence

fidus -a -um	faithful, loyal
figo, figere, fixi, fixum	to fix, affix
fines, -ium *m.pl.*	territory, land
finio, finire, finivi, finitum	to finish, end
finitimus -a -um	neighbouring
***flamma, -ae** *f.*	flame
flos, floris *m.*	flower
***flumen, -inis** *n.*	river
fluo, fluere, fluxi, fluxum	to flow, fall
fluvius, -i *m.*	river
focus, -i *m.*	hearth, pyre
foedo, foedare, foedavi, foedatum	to defile, foul
***foedus, -eris** *n.*	treaty
for, fari, fatus sum	to speak
foris, -is *f.*	door, entrance
forma, -ae *f.*	shape, beauty
fors (*adv.*)	perhaps
***forte** (*adv.*)	by chance
***fortis -e**	brave
***fortuna, -ae** *f.*	fortune (also personified)
fragor, -oris *m.*	clamour
fraxinus, -i *f.*	ash-tree
fremo, fremere, fremui, fremitum	to roar, shout out, speak loudly
frena, -orum *n.pl.*	bridles
fretus -a -um + *abl.*	relying on, trusting in
frigidus -a -um	cold
frons, frondis *f.*	foliage
***frustra** (*adv.*)	in vain
***fuga, -ae** *f.*	flight
***fugio, fugere, fugi, fugitum**	to flee, run away, flee from

fulcio, fulcire, fulsi, fultum	to support, prop up
fulgeo, fulgere, fulsi	to shine, gleam, be resplendent
fulgor, -oris *m.*	brightness, splendour
fulvus -a -um	golden, tawny
funda, -ae *f.*	sling
***fundo, fundere, fudi, fusum**	to pour, lay low
funereus -a –um	funereal, for a funeral
funus, -eris *n.*	death
furo, furere, furui	to be mad, furious
furtim (*adv.*)	furtively, stealthily
furtum, -i *n.*	trick, stratagem
galea, -ae *f.*	helmet
***gaudium, -i** *n.*	joy, pleasure
gelidus -a -um	chill
geminus -a -um	twin, a pair of
gemitus, -us *m.*	groan
gemo, gemere, gemui, gemitum	to groan
genitor, -oris *m.*	father
***gens, -ntis** *f.*	race, people
***gero, gerere, gessi, gestum**	to wage (war), carry, wear
gloria, -ae *f.*	glory
Gortynius -a -um	from Gortys, Cretan
gradior, gradi, gressus sum	to go
gramineus -a -um	grassy
grandis -e	large, abundant
grates *f.pl.*	thanks
gratus -a -um	grateful
gremium, -i *n.*	lap, bosom
gressus, -us *m.*	step
grus, gruis *f.*	crane
gutta, -ae *f.*	drop

habena, -ae *f.*	thong, rein
*habeo, habere, habui, habitum	to have
habilis -e	handy, manageable
hac (*adv.*)	here
hactenus (*adv.*)	thus far, until now
haereo, haerere, haesi, haesum	to stick, cling (to)
Harpalycus, -i *m.*	Harpalycus
haruspex, -icis *m.*	soothsayer
*hasta, -ae *f.*	spear, javelin
hastile, -is *n.*	javelin
*haud	not
hei!	alas!
hiatus, -us *m.*	gape
*hic (*adv.*)	here, at this point
*hic, haec, hoc	this
*hinc (*adv.*)	from here
Hippolyte, -es (*acc.* -en) *f.*	Hippolyte
Hippotades, -ae (*acc.* -en) *m.*	descendant of Hippotes
*homo, -inis *m.*	man, human
*honos, -oris *m.*	honour
horrendus -a -um	awe-inspiring
horrens, -ntis	bristly, thorny
horreo, horrere, horrui	to bristle
horridus -a -um	terrible
*hortor, hortari, hortatus sum	to urge, encourage
*hospes, -itis *m.*	host, guest
hospitium, -i *n.*	hospitality, friendship
hostia, -ae *f.*	sacrificial victim
hostilis -e	hostile, of the enemy
*hostis, -is *m.*	enemy
*huc (*adv.*)	to this place

humo, humare, humavi, humatum	to bury
***humus, -i** f.	ground, earth
hyacinthus, -i m.	hyacinth, lily
hymenaeus, -i m.	wedding
***iaceo, iacere, iacui,**	to lie
iaculum, -i n.	javelin
***iam** (adv.)	now, already, by now
Iapyx, -igis	Iapygian, South Italian
***idem, eadem, idem**	the same
ignarus -a -um	unaware, ignorant, unready
ignavia, -ae f.	idleness, cowardice
igneus -a -um	like fire
***ignis, -is** m.	fire
ignotus -a -um	unknown, unfamiliar
Iliades, -um f.pl.	Trojan women
***ille, illa, illud**	that; he, she, it
imber, -bris m.	rainstorm
imitor, imitari, imitatus sum	to imitate
immanis -e	huge, immense
immaturus -a -um	untimely, premature
immensus -a -um	immense
immisceo, immiscere, immiscui, immixtum	to mingle, intermingle
immitto, immittere, immisi, immissum	to cast, let fly
immugio, immugire, immugi(v)i	to roar, resound
immulgeo, immulgere	to milk
***impedio, impedire, impedivi, impeditum**	to hinder

*imperium, -i *n.*	empire
*impero, imperare, imperavi, imperatum	to order
implico, implicare, implicui, implicitum	to involve, bind, wrap round
improbus -a -um	wicked, shameless
impune (*adv.*)	safely, with impunity
imus -a -um	the bottom of, the depths of, deepest
*in + *abl.*	in, on
*in + *acc.*	into, onto, against
inanis -e	empty, vain
incautus -a -um	reckless
*incendo, incendere, incendi, incensum	to set on fire
*incipio, incipere, incepi, inceptum	to begin
incumbo, incumbere, incubui, incubitum	to fall upon, attack
incurro, incurrere, incurri, incursum	to attack
indefessus -a -um	tireless
indico, indicere, indixi, indictum	to proclaim
indignor, indignari, indignatus sum	to complain
indignus -a -um	unworthy, undeserved, cruel
induo, induere, indui, indutum	to dress in, put on
inermis -e	unarmed
iners, -rtis	lacking movement, lacking skill
infans, -ntis *m/f.*	infant, baby
infaustus -a -um	unlucky, unfavourable

infelix, -icis	unfortunate, unhappy
infensus -a -um	hostile
inferiae, -arum *f.pl.*	offerings
***infero, inferre, intuli, inlatum**	to carry in, bring in, move forward
infodio, infodere, infodi, infossum	to bury
***ingens, -ntis**	huge
inglorius -a -um	without glory
ingravo, ingravare, ingravavi, ingravatum	to aggravate, make worse
inhumatus -a -um	unburied
inicio, inicere, inieci, iniectum	to inspire, cause
***inimicus -a -um**	hostile, of the enemy
inlacrimo, inlacrimare, inlacrimavi, inlacrimatum	to lament
inno, innare, innavi, innatum	to swim in
innumerus -a -um	countless
***inquam** (defective verb)	to say
inritus -a -um	useless
***insidiae, -arum** *f.pl.*	ambush
insignia, -ium *n.pl.*	trappings
***insignis -e**	conspicuous
insisto, insistere, institi	to plant
insono, insonare, insonui	to resound
inspoliatus -a -um	not despoiled, not pillaged
instigo, instigare, instigavi, instigatum	to goad, incite
insuper (*adv.*)	in addition
insurgo, insurgere, insurrexi, insurrectum	to rise
intemeratus -a -um	pure, undefiled

*inter + *acc.*	between, among
*interea (*adv.*)	meanwhile
intersum, interesse, interfui (+ *dat.*)	to take part in
inumbro, inumbrare, inumbravi, inumbratum	to shade, cover
inverto, invertere, inverti, inversum	to invert, turn round
invideo, invidere, invidi, invisum	to begrudge
invidia, -ae *f.*	hatred, envy
inviso, invisere, invisi, invisum	to visit
invisus -a -um	hateful, hated
*ipse -a, -um	(anyone's) self
*ira, irae *f.*	anger
iste, ista, istud	that (of yours)
*ita (*adv.*)	thus, so, in this way, as follows
Italia, -ae *f.*	Italy
Italis, -idis *f.*	an Italian woman
Italus, -i *m.*	an Italian
*iter, itineris *n.*	journey, route, way
*iubeo, iubere, iussi, iussum	to order
iugulo, iugulare, iugulavi, iugulatum	to cut the throat of, slaughter
iugulum, -i *n.*	throat
iugum, -i *n.*	yoke, ridge
Iulus, -i *m.*	Iulus, Ascanius
*iungo, iungere, iunxi, iunctum	to join, unite
iustitia, -ae *f.*	justice
iuvat, iuvare, iuvit (*impersonal*)	it pleases
iuvencus, -i *m.*	bullock
*iuvenis, -is *m.*	young man, youth

*lābor, labi, lapsus sum	to glide down, fall
*lăbor, -oris *m.*	work, toil
labrum, -i *n.*	lip
lac, lactis *n.*	milk
lacertus, -i *m.*	arm
lacesso, lacessere, lacessivi, lacessitum	to challenge, provoke
lacrima, -ae *f.*	tear
lacrimo, lacrimare, lacrimavi, lacrimatum	to cry
laetitia, -ae *f.*	joy
*laetus -a -um	happy, joyful
langueo, languere	to droop
Larina, -ae *f.*	Larina
Latini, -orum *m.pl.*	the Latins, people of Latium
Latinus -a -um	Latin
Latinus, -i *m.*	Latinus (the king)
Latium, -i *n.*	Latium
Latonia, -ae *f.*	daughter of Latona, Diana
*lātus -a -um	broad
*lătus, -eris *n.*	side
Laurens, -ntis	of Laurentum, Laurentine
*laus, -dis *f.*	praise
laxo, laxare, laxavi, laxatum	to open
*lego, legere, legi, lectum	to choose
*lentus -a -um	tough, flexible, drooping
letalis -e	lethal, mortal
letum, -i *n.*	death
lēvis -e	smooth
*lĕvis -e	light
liber, -bri *m.*	bark

libro, librare, libravi, libratum	to balance, poise
limen, liminis *n.*	threshold, doorway, entrance
linquo, linquere, liqui	to let go of
Liris, -is (*acc.* **-im**), *m.*	Liris
***litus, -oris** *n.*	shore
***locus, -i** *m.*	place
longe (*adv.*)	far, from afar
***longus -a -um**	long
luceo, lucere, luxi	to shine, be light, be bright
luctor, luctari, luctatus sum	to struggle
luctus, -us *m.*	lamentation, mourning, grief
lucus, -i *m.*	grove, wood
lumen, -inis *n.*	light, eye
lunatus -a -um	lunate, crescent-shaped
lupus, -i *m.*	wolf
lustro, lustrare, lustravi, lustratum	to go round, watch
lustrum, -i *n.*	den, woodland
***lux, lucis** *f.*	light, daylight, dawn
Lycius -a -um	Lycian
macto, mactare, mactavi, mactatum	to sacrifice
Maeonidae, -arum *m.pl.*	the Maeonidae, Etruscans
maereo, maerere	to mourn
maestus -a -um	sad, sorrowful, mourning
***magnus -a -um**	large, great
mala, -ae *f.*	jaw
mamma, -ae *f.*	teat
mandatum, -i *n.*	command, commission
***mando, mandare, mandavi, mandatum**	to entrust, commit

mando, mandere, mandi, mansum	to chew
*maneo, manere, mansi, mansum	to wait, await, remain
*manus, -us *f.*	hand, band or group
Mars, -tis *m.*	Mars, war (personified)
Martius -a -um	of Mars, warlike, martial
*mater, -tris *f.*	mother
medium, -i *n.*	middle
*medius -a -um	middle, middle of
memor, -oris	mindful, remembering, aware
*mens, mentis *f.*	mind, decision
mensa, -ae *f.*	table
mereo, merere, merui, meritum	to earn, win
mergo, mergere, mersi, mersum	to drown, overwhelm
merito (*adv.*)	deservedly
meritum, -i *n.*	just deserts, meritorious action
Messapus, -i *m.*	Messapus
Metabus, -i *m.*	Metabus
metuo, metuere, metui, metutum	to fear
*metus, -us *m.*	fear
*meus -a -um	my
Mezentius, -i *m.*	Mezentius
*miles, -itis *m.*	soldier, troops
militia, -ae *f.*	warfare
mille	thousand
ministra, -ae *f.*	attendant
ministro, ministrare, ministravi, ministratum	to supply
minus (*adv.*)	less

*miror, mirari, miratus sum	to wonder at, marvel at, admire
misceo, miscere, miscui, mixtum	to mix, mingle
*miser -era -erum	wretched, poor, pitiful
miserabilis -e	pitiful
miseror, miserari, miseratus sum	to pity
*mitto, mittere, misi, missum	to send
*modo (*adv.*)	now, just now, recently, only
*moenia, -ium *n.pl.*	city walls, walled town
moles, -is *f.*	mass
mollis -e	soft, gentle
*moneo, monere, monui, monitum	to warn, advise
*mons, montis *m.*	mountain
*mora, -ae *f.*	delay
*morior, mori, mortuus sum	to die
*moror, morari, moratus sum	to delay, prolong
*mors, mortis *f.*	death (also personified)
mortales, -ium *m.pl.*	mortals
*mos, moris *m.*	custom
*moveo, movere, movi, motum	to move, stir
mucro, -onis *m.*	point, spear-tip
muliebris -e	of a woman
*multus -a -um	much, *pl.* many
*munus, -eris *n.*	duty, gift, rite, offering
*murus, -i *m.*	wall
*muto, mutare, mutavi, mutatum	to change
*nam	for
namque	for

nata, -ae *f.*	daughter
natus, -i *m.*	son
***ne**	lest, so that not
ne qui, qua, quod	lest any, so that no
***nec, neque**	nor, neither
nemus, -oris *n.*	grove, wood
nequiquam (*adv.*)	in vain
niger, nigra, nigrum	black
nigresco, nigrescere	to grow dark
***nihil, nil**	nothing
niveus -a -um	snowy, snow-white
nocturnus -a -um	nocturnal, at night
nodus, -i *m.*	knot
***nomen, -inis** *n.*	name
***non**	not
non iam	no longer
***nos, nostri**	we
***noster -tra -trum**	our
***notus -a -um**	well-known, traditional
Notus, -i *m.*	South Wind
***novus -a -um**	new; (sup.) last
***nox, noctis** *f.*	night
nubes, -is *f.*	cloud
***nullus -a -um**	no, not any
***numerus, -i** *m.*	number
***numquam** (*adv.*)	never
***nunc**	now, as it is
***nuntio, nuntiare, nuntiavi, nuntiatum**	to announce
nurus, -us *f.*	daughter-in-law
nutrio, nutrire, nutrivi, nutritum	to rear, feed
nympha, -ae *f.*	nymph

ob + acc.	on account of, because of
obnubo, obnubere, obnupsi, obnuptum	to veil, cover
oborior, oboriri, obortus sum	to well up, rise
obruo, obruere, obrui, obrutum	to overwhelm
observo, observare, observavi, observatum	to observe
obsido, obsidere	to blockade, occupy
obstipesco, obstipescere, obstipui	to be astonished
obtentus, -us *m.*	canopy
obumbro, obumbrare, obumbravi, obumbratum	to cloak, defend, protect
obuncus -a -um	hooked
obvius -a -um + *dat.*	to meet
*occido, occidere, occidi, occisum	to kill
occurro, occurrere, occurri, occursum + *dat.*	to run up to, run to meet, face
Oceanus, -i *m.*	the (River of) Ocean
*oculus, -i *m.*	eye
*odium, -i *n.*	hate, hatred
olea, -ae *f.*	olive, olive-wood
olens, -ntis	fragrant
*olim (*adv.*)	once
olor, -oris *m.*	swan
Olympus, -i *m.*	(Mt) Olympus
omen, -inis *n.*	omen
omnipotens, -ntis	all-powerful
*omnis -e	all, every
onero, onerare, oneravi, oneratum	to pile up

*onus, -eris *n*.	burden
operio, operire, operui, opertum	to cover
Opis, -is (*acc.* -im) *f*.	Opis
*oppidum, -i *n*.	town
oppono, opponere, opposui, oppositum	to expose
opto, optare, optavi, optatum	to wish for
*opus, -eris *n*.	work, task
orator, -oris *m*.	speaker
orbus -a -um + *abl.*	bereft of
*ordo, -inis *m*.	line, row
ornus, -i *f*.	mountain-ash
Ornytus, -i *m*.	Ornytus
*oro, orare, oravi, oratum	to beg, ask
orsus, -us *m*.	beginning
*os, oris *n*.	face, mouth
os, ossis *n*.	bone
ostrum, -i *n*.	purple dye
ovans, -ntis	triumphant
Pagasus, -i *m*.	Pagasus
palla, -ae *f*.	robe, dress
Pallas, -antis *m*.	Pallas
palma, -ae *f*.	palm
palor, palari, palatus sum	to straggle
pango, pangere, pepigi, pactum	to agree, make an agreement
papilla, -ae *f*.	breast
*par, paris	equal, the same
*parco, parcere, peperci, parsum + *dat.*	to spare
*parens, -ntis *m/f*.	parent

*pario, parere, peperi, partum	to give birth to, create
*paro, parare, paravi, paratum	to prepare
Parrhasius -a -um	of Parrhasia, Parrhasian
*pars, partis *f.*	part, others
partim (*adv.*)	partly
partior, partiri, partitus sum	to share
*parvus -a -um	small, little
pasco, pascere, pavi, pastum	to feed, nourish
pastor, -oris *m.*	shepherd
pateo, patere, patui	to be open, gape open
*pater, -tris *m.*	father, ancestor
paternus -a -um	paternal, of one's father, ancestral, native
*patria, -ae *f.*	fatherland, homeland
patrius -a -um	native
*paulatim (*adv.*)	gradually
pavito, pavitare	to tremble with fear
*pax, pacis *f.*	peace
pectus, -oris *n.*	breast
pecus, -udis *f.*	cow, sheep
*pedes, -itis *m.*	foot-soldier
pellis, -is *f.*	skin, hide
*pello, pellere, pepuli, pulsum	to put to flight, beat, drive, defeat
pelta, -ae *f.*	light shield
pendeo, pendere, pependi	to hang
Penthesilea, -ae *f.*	Penthesilea
*per + *acc.*	through, along
*perdo, perdere, perdidi, perditum	to lose
peregrinus -a -um	foreign, exotic
pererro, pererrare, pererravi, pererratum	to try, wander through

perfero, perferre, pertuli, perlatum	to carry through, deliver
perfodio, perfodere, perfodi, perfossum	to pierce
perfundo, perfundere, perfudi, perfusum	to soak
pergo, pergere, perrexi, perrectum	to proceed
***periculum, -i** *n.*	danger
perimo, perimere, peremi, peremptum	to kill
***pes, pedis** *m.*	foot
pestis, -is *f.*	pest, plague
***peto, petere, petivi, petitum**	to attack, seek, make for, ask for
phalanx, -ngis *f.*	phalanx, battle formation
pharetra -ae *f.*	quiver
pharetratus -a -um	bearing a quiver
Phoebus, -i *m.*	Phoebus, Apollo
Phryges, -um *m.pl.*	Phrygians, Trojans
Phrygii, -orum *m.pl.*	Phrygians, Trojans
pietas, -atis *f.*	piety, dutifulness, faith
pineus -a -um	pine, of pine-wood
pingo, pingere, pinxi, pictum	to paint; (with *acu*) embroider
pinguis -e	fat
pinus, -us *f.*	pine-tree
pius -a -um	dutiful
plango, plangere, planxi, planctum	to mourn, lament
planta, -ae *f.*	sole of the foot
plaustrum, -i *n.*	cart, wagon
***plenus -a -um**	full, loaded
pluma, -ae *f.*	feather

poculum, -i *n.*	cup, wine-cup
*poenas do, dare, dedi, datum	to pay the penalty, be punished
pollex, -icis *m.*	thumb
polum, -i *n.*	sky
pompa, -ae *f.*	procession
*pono, ponere, posui, positum	to place, put, set aside, lay down
*porta, -ae *f.*	gate
*porto, portare, portavi, portatum	to carry
*posco, poscere, poposci	to demand, call on
*possum, posse, potui	to be able
*post (*adv.*)	behind, after
*post + *acc.*	behind, after
*postquam	after, when
*postremus -a -um	last
potis (*indecl.*)	able
*potius (*adv.*)	rather, instead
prae + *acc.*	in front of
praecedo, praecedere, praecessi, praecessum	to go in front, lead the way
praecipito, praecipitare, praecipitavi, praecipitatum	to urge
praecipuus -a -um	principal
*praeda, -ae *f.*	booty, spoils
praedives, -itis	very wealthy
praedulcis -e	very sweet
praefigo, praefigere, praefixi, praefixum	to fix in front
praemitto, praemittere, praemisi, praemissum	to send ahead
*praemium, -i *n.*	spoils
praenuntia, -ae *f.*	foreteller, harbinger

*praesidium, -i *n.*	protection, defence
praesumo, praesumere, praesumpsi, praesumptum	to anticipate. be ready for
*praeterea (*adv.*)	furthermore, in addition
*precor, precari, precatus sum	to pray, beg for, ask for
premo, premere, pressi, pressum	to press, pursue closely
prex, -ecis *f.*	prayer, plea
primitiae, -arum *f.pl.*	first-fruits
*primus -a -um	first
*prior, -oris	first, superior
*prius (*adv.*)	previously, first
*prius quam	before
Privernum, -i *n.*	Privernum
*pro +*abl.*	for, on behalf of, instead of
procella, -ae *f.*	strong wind, gale
*procul (*adv.*)	far off
procumbo, procumbere, procubui, procubitum	to bend over
*proelium, -i *n.*	battle
proicio, proicere, proieci, proiectum	to throw forward
promissum, -i *n.*	promise
*promitto, promittere, promisi, promissum	to promise
*prope (*adv.*)	near
propinquus -a -um	neighbouring, nearby
prosequor, prosequi, prosecutus sum	to accompany, present, honour with
pruna, -ae *f.*	burning coal
pubes, -is *f.*	youth, young people, the young
pudendus -a -um	shameful

*puer, pueri *m.*	boy
puerilis -e	of a child, child-sized
*pugna, -ae *f.*	fight, battle
pugnator, -oris *m.*	fighter
pugnus, -i *m.*	fist
pulso, pulsare, pulsavi, pulsatum	to pound, beat
purpureus -a -um	purple, red
*puto, putare, putavi, putatum	to think
pyra, -ae *f.*	funeral pyre
qua	where
quacumque	wherever
*quaero, quaerere, quaesivi, quaesitum	to seek, look for
*qualis -e	just as, just like
*quamquam	although
quando	since
quandoquidem	since, seeing that
*quantus -a -um	how much, how great
quatio, quatere, quassum	to shake, brandish, scour, harass, reconnoitre, trample
quercus, -us *f.*	oak-tree
quernus -a -um	oak, of oak wood
*qui, quae, quod	who, which
quicumque, quaecumque, quodcumque	whoever, whatever
*quid?	why?
*quidem (*adv.*)	indeed, however
quin (*adv.*)	indeed
quinam, quaenam, quodnam	who, which
*quisque, quaeque, quodque	each

quo?	to what purpose?
***quod**	because
***quod si**	but if
quondam (*adv.*)	once, previously
***quoque** (*adv.*)	also
***quot?**	how many?
ramus, -i *m.*	branch
rapidus -a -um	rapid, fast-flowing
***rapio, rapere, rapui, raptum**	to grab, seize
recedo, recedere, recessi, recessum	to recede, wither, retreat
***recipio, recipere, recepi, receptum**	to take back
redarguo, redarguere, redargui	to refute
***reddo, reddere, reddidi, redditum**	to return, restore, hand back
reditus, -us *m.*	return
redux, -ucis	returned
***refero, referre, rettuli, relatum**	to bring back, refer, relate, give back
***reficio, reficere, refeci, refectum**	to restore, revive
regia, -ae *f.*	palace, abode of a king
***regina, -ae** *f.*	queen
***regnum, -i** *n.*	kingdom, realm
***relinquo, relinquere, reliqui, relictum**	to leave, leave behind
remeo, remeare, remeavi	to return
remitto, remittere, remisi, remissum	to send back
remulceo, remulcere, remulsi, remulsum	to droop

repleo, replere, replevi, repletum	to fill
repono, reponere, reposui, repositum	to set down, restore
reporto, reportare, reportavi, reportatum	to bring back
repugno, repugnare, repugnavi, repugnatum	to fight back
***res, rei** *f.*	thing, matter, business
resto, restare, restiti	to remain, be left
revolvo, revolvere, revolvi, revolutum	to roll backwards
***rex, regis** *m.*	king
rigeo, rigere	to be stiff
rimor, rimari, rimatus sum	to search for, probe for
***ripa, -ae** *f.*	bank
rivus, -i *m.*	stream
robur, -oris *n.*	oak-tree, timber, strength
***rogo, rogare, rogavi, rogatum**	to ask, ask for
rogus, -i *m.*	pyre
roro, rorare, roravi, roratum	to drip
rostrum, -i *n.*	bill, beak
rota, -ae *f.*	wheel
rudimentum, -i *n.*	first attempt
***rumpo, rumpere, rupi, ruptum**	to burst
ruo, ruere, rui, rutum	to rush, rake up (211), fall down
Rutuli, -orum *m.pl.*	the Rutuli, Rutulians
Rutulus -a -um	Rutulian
sacer -cra -crum	sacred
***sacerdos, -otis** *m.*	priest

sacrum, -i *n.*	sacred rite, sacrifice
saetiger -era -erum	bristly
***saevus -a -um**	cruel, savage
sagitta, -ae *f.*	arrow
salve	hail, greetings
sanctus -a -um	virtuous, sacred, holy
***sanguis, -inis** *m.*	blood
sator, -oris *m.*	creator, father
saucius -a -um	wounded
saxum -i *n.*	stone, rock
scindo, scindere, scidi, scissum	to split
***se, sese**	himself, herself, itself, themselves
***secundus -a -um**	favourable, propitious
securis, -is (*acc.* **-im**) *f.*	axe
secus (*adv.*)	otherwise, differently
***sed**	but
sedeo, sedere, sedi, sessum	to sit, settle, become fixed
***sedes, -is** *f.*	seat, home, hall
segnis, -e	slow, sluggish
***semper** (*adv.*)	always
semustus -a -um	half-burnt
senecta, -ae *f.*	old age
***senex -is**	old, elderly; (noun) old man
seni -ae -a	six, six each
***sententia, -ae** *f.*	feeling, opinion
sequestra, -ae *f.*	protectress, guarantor
***sequor, sequi, secutus sum**	to follow
serpens, -ntis *m.*	snake
***servo, servare, servavi, servatum**	to save, protect, watch over, keep alive
seu	whether, or
sex	six

*si	if
si quando	whenever
si qui, si qua, si quod	if any
sibilo, sibilare	to hiss
*sic (*adv.*)	thus, so, in this way, as follows
Sidonius -a -um	Sidonian, from Sidon
sidus, -eris *n.*	star
*signum, -i *n.*	standard, sign
silens, -ntis	silent, in silence
*silva, -ae *f.*	wood
silvestris -e	from the forest
*simul (*adv.*)	at the same time
*sinistra, -ae *f.*	the left side
*sino, sinere, sivi, situm	to allow
sinuosus -a -um	winding, sinuous
sinus, -us *m.*	lap, fold
*sive	whether, or
socer, -eri *m.*	father-in-law
socius -a -um	allied
*socius, -i *m.*	ally, friend, companion, comrade
solacium -i *n.*	solace, comfort
solidus -a -um	solid
*solus -a -um	only, alone, sole, lonely
solvo, solvere, solvi, solutum	to fulfil, pay off, loosen, untie
sonitus, -us *m.*	sound, noise
sono, sonare, sonui, sonitum	to sound, resound
Soracte, -is *n.*	Soracte
*soror, -oris *f.*	sister
sors, -tis *f.*	lot, chance, fate
sospes, -itis	safe, unhurt
spargo, spargere, sparsi, sparsum	to scatter, sprinkle, spatter

sparus, -i *m.*	hunting-spear
***specto, spectare, spectavi, spectatum**	to watch
***spes, spei** *f.*	hope
spiculum, -i *n.*	arrow
spolio, spoliare, spoliavi, spoliatum	to despoil
***spolium, -i** *n.*	spoils, booty
sponte(*adv.*)	of one's own free will, voluntarily
spumo, spumare, spumavi, spumatum	to foam, be in full spate
squama, -ae *f.*	scale
stella, -ae *f.*	star
sterno, sternere, stravi, stratum	to throw down, lay low; (pass.) collapse
stimulus, -i *m.*	goad
stipo, stipare, stipavi, stipatum	to press, pack together
***sto, stare, steti, statum**	I stand
stramen, -inis *n.*	straw, bed
strideo, stridere, stridi	to whistle, whirr
struo, struere, struxi, structum	to build, construct
Strymonius -a -um	of the river Strymon, Strymonian
***studium, -i** *n.*	enthusiasm
***sub** + *abl.*	under, down in, down among
***sub** + *acc.*	down to
subeo, subire, subii, subitum	to come up, approach
suber, -eris *n.*	cork
subicio, subicere, subieci, subiectum	to place under, throw under
***subito** (*adv.*)	suddenly
subitus -a -um	sudden

subligo, subligare, subligavi, subligatum	to fasten
sublimis -e	high up, distinguished
subsisto, subsistere, substiti	to stop, halt
subvecto, subvectare, subvectavi, subvectatum	to bring up, transport
succedo, succedere, successi, successum	to go under, be placed under, draw near to, be successful, take over
suffundo, suffundere, suffudi, suffusum	to stumble
***sum, esse, fui**	to be
***summus -a -um**	the top of, the tip of, greatest, highest
super (*adv.*)	on top, above
super + *acc.*	over, above
superbus -a -um	proud, arrogant
superi, -orum *m.pl.*	the gods above
***supero, superare, superavi, superatum**	to cross over
superstes, -itis	surviving
***supersum, superesse, superfui**	to remain
superus -a -um	above, of heaven
supplex, -icis	submissive, begging, in supplication
suppono, supponere, supposui, suppositum	to place beneath
supra (*adv.*)	above
supra + *acc.*	beyond
supremus -a -um	last
***surgo, surgere, surrexi, surrectum**	to rise
sus, suis *m.*	pig, boar

*suscipio, suscipere, suscepi, susceptum	to take up, catch
suscito, suscitare, suscitavi, suscitatum	to rouse
suspendo, suspendere, suspendi, suspensum	to hang
sustento, sustentare, sustentavi, sustentatum	to support
sustineo, sustinere, sustinui, sustentum	to ward off
*suus -a -um	his, her, its, their own
*tacitus -a -um	silent
*talis -e	such, the following
*tandem (*adv.*)	finally, at last
*tantus -a -um	so great, such a great
Tarchon, -onis *m.*	Tarchon
tardo, tardare, tardavi, tardatum	to delay, slow down
Tarpeia, -ae *f.*	Tarpeia
*tectum, -i *n.*	roof, house
tegmen, -inis *n.*	covering
*tego, tegere, texi, tectum	to cover, protect, surround
tela, -ae *f.*	warp (on a loom)
tellus, -uris *f.*	earth
*telum, -i *n.*	weapon, spear, javelin
*templum, -i *n.*	temple
tempto, temptare, temptavi, temptatum	to try, test
*tempus, -oris *n.*	time
tendo, tendere, tetendi, tentum	to proceed, direct one's course, extend

tenebrae, tenebrarum *f.pl.*	darkness
***teneo, tenere, tenui, tentum**	to hold, keep
tener -era -erum	tender
tenuis -e	thin, fine
tepidus -a -um	warm, tepid
ter (*adv.*)	three times
teres, -etis	smooth
Tereus, -eos (*acc.* **-ea**) *m.*	Tereus
***tergum, -i** *n.*	back
***terra, -ae** *f.*	earth, land, ground
tertius -a -um	third
testor, testari, testatus sum	to testify, witness, call on to witness
Teucri, -orum *m.pl.*	the Trojans
texo, texere, texui, textum	to weave
Thermodon, -ontis *m.*	river Thermodon
thorax, -acis *m.*	breast-plate
Threicius -a -um	Thracian
tibia, -ae *f.*	flute, pipe
Tiburtes, -um *m.pl.*	people of Tibur, Tiburtines
Tiburtus, -i *m.*	Tiburtus
tigris, -idis *f.*	tigress
***timeo, timere, timui**	to fear
***timor, -oris** *m.*	fear
***tollo, tollere, sustuli, sublatum**	to raise, remove
torqueo, torquere, torsi, tortum	to wield
torus, -i *m.*	couch, bed
***tot**	so many
***totus -a -um**	whole, all
traicio, traicere, traieci, traiectum	to pierce, transfix
trames, -itis *m.*	path

transverbero, transverberare, transverberavi, transverberatum	to pierce, transfix
trepidus -a -um	anxious
***tristis -e**	sad
triumphus, -i *m.*	triumph
Trivia, -ae *f.*	Trivia, Diana
Troes, -um *m.pl.*	the Trojans
Troia, -ae *f.*	Troy
Troianus -a -um	Trojan
tropaeum, -i *n.*	trophy
Tros, Trois *m.*	a Trojan
truncus -a -um	broken
truncus, -i *m.*	trunk (of a tree)
***tu, tui**	you
tuba, -ae *f.*	trumpet
Tulla, -ae *f.*	Tulla
***tum** (*adv.*)	then
tumultus, -us *m.*	commotion, tumult
tumulus, -i *m.*	mound
tunc (*adv.*)	then
tundo, tundere, tutudi, tunsum	to beat
***turba, -ae** *f.*	crowd, throng
turbidus -a -um	violent, frantic
turbo, -inis *m.*	whirlwind
turbo, turbare, turbavi, turbatum	to trouble, distract
turma, -ae *f.*	squadron of cavalry
Turnus, -i *m.*	Turnus
***tuus -a -um**	your
Tyrrheni, -orum *m.pl.*	the Etruscans
Tyrrhenus -a -um	Etruscan

uber, -eris *n.*	udder
*ubi	when, where
*ullus -a -um	any
ultrix, -icis	avenging
ululatus, -us *m.*	wailing, shrieking
ululo, ululare, ululavi, ululatum	to wail, cry out with joy
umbra, -ae *f.*	shade, spirit (of the dead), darkness
umecto, umectare, umectavi, umectatum	to wet
umerus, -i *m.*	shoulder
umidus -a -um	damp, dewy
*unda, -ae *f.*	wave, water
*undique (*adv.*)	on all sides, all round
unguis, -is *m.*	nail, talon
unus -a -um	one
*urbs, -is *f.*	city, town
urgeo, urgere, ursi	to press upon, close in on, attack
*ut + *indic.*	when, as
*ut + *subjunc.*	to, in order to, that
uterus, -i *m.*	belly
vaco, vacare, vacavi, vacatum	to be left open
vado, vadere	to go
vale	farewell
*validus -a -um	strong
vanus -a -um	empty
varius -a -um	various, varied
vastus -a -um	vast, extensive
vates, -is *m.*	prophet
vecto, vectare, vectavi, vectatum	to carry, convey

*veho, vehere, vexi, vectum	to convey (passive = to travel, ride)
vello, vellere, vulsi, vulsum	to pull up, pluck
velo, velare, velavi, velatum	to veil, overshadow
velox, -ocis	swift
*velut	just as, just like
venator, -oris *m.*	hunter
venatrix, -icis *f.*	huntress
venia, -ae *f.*	pardon, indulgence, permission
*venio, venire, veni, ventum	to come
Venulus, -i *m.*	Venulus
Venus, -eris *f.*	Venus, love
verbero, verberare, verberavi, verberatum	to beat
*vero (*adv.*)	however, indeed
verso, versare, versavi, versatum	to turn over, writhe, twist
vertex, -icis *m.*	top, head
*verto, vertere, verti, versum	to turn, reverse, turn back
verum	but
vestigium, -i *n.*	footprint
*vestis, -is *f.*	clothing, garment
vetustus -a -um	old, ancient
*via, -ae *f.*	way, road
vicissim (*adv.*)	in turn
*victor, -oris *m.*	victor
victrix, -icis	victorious
*video, videre, vidi, visum	to see
vimen, -inis *n.*	pliant twig, osier
vincio, vincire, vinxi, vinctum	to bind, tie
*vinco, vincere, vici, victum	to defeat, conquer
viola, -ae *f.*	violet
violo, violare, violavi, violatum	to violate, harm

*vir, viri *m.*	man
virga, -ae *f.*	twig
virgineus -a -um	of a maiden
virginitas, -atis *f.*	virginity
virgo, -inis *f.*	maiden
*virtus, -utis *f.*	virtue, courage
*vis, *pl.* vires, virium *f.*	force, violence; (pl.) strength
*vita, -ae *f.*	life
*vivo, vivere, vixi, victum	to live
*vivus -a -um	alive, living
*vix (*adv.*)	scarcely, with difficulty
*voco, vocare, vocavi, vocatum	to call, summon
volito, volitare	to charge about
*volo, velle, volui	I wish, want
volo, volare, volavi, volatum	to fly
Volsci, -orum *m.pl.*	the Volsci, Volscians
volucer -cris -cre	swift
volumen, -inis *n.*	coil
vomo, vomere, vomui, vomitum	to vomit, spew out
*vos, vestri	you
votum, -i *n.*	vow
voveo, vovere, vovi, votum	to vow, promise, dedicate
*vox, vocis *f.*	voice, word
*vulnus, -eris *n.*	wound

Printed in Great Britain
by Amazon